Reconciliation and Peace in South Sudan

A Christian Perspective

Levi Lukadi Noah

Langham

MONOGRAPHS

© 2012 by Levi Lukadi Noah

Published 2012 by Langham Monographs,
an imprint of Langham Creative Projects

Bishop Tucker School of Divinity & Theology Uganda, Dissertation 2006

Langham Partnership
PO Box 296, Carlisle, Cumbria, CA3 9WZ
www.langham.org

ISBNs:
978-1-907713-31-6   print
978-1-907713-32-3   Mobi
978-1-907713-33-0   ePub

British Library Cataloguing-in-Publication Data
Lukadi, Levi.
  Reconciliation and peace in South Sudan : a Christian
  perspective.
  1. Christianity and politics--Sudan. 2. Reconciliation--
  Religious aspects--Christianity. 3. Peace-building--
  Religious aspects--Christianity. 4. Sudan--History--
  Civil War, 1983-2005--Peace. 5. South Sudan--Social
  conditions--21st century. 6. South Sudan--Politics and
  government--2005-2011. 7. South Sudan--Politics and
  government--2011-
  I. Title
  261.7'09624-dc23

  ISBN-13: 9781907713316

Cover and Book Design: projectluz.com

Contents

Acknowledgements   vii

Abstract   ix

Chapter 1   1

Introduction

1.1 Background to the Study   1

1.2 Statement of Problem and Definition of Terms   5

   1.2.1 Statement of the Problem   5

   1.2.2 Definition of Terms   5

1.3 Hypothesis   5

1.4 Justification of the Study   6

1.5 Significance of the Study   7

1.6 Specific Immediate Objectives   7

1.7 The Scope of the Study   8

1.8 Methodology   8

1.9 Limitations   10

1.10 Literature Review   10

   1.10.1 Socio-Political Reconciliation and Peace   10

   1.10.2 Biblical Reconciliation and Peace   13

   1.10.3 Reconciliation and Peace in South Sudan Context   14

Chapter 2   19

Background to Sudan's Conflict

2.1 Introduction   19

2.2 Historical Background   19

2.3 Political Factors   22

2.4 Religious Factors   26

2.5 Socio-economic Factors   27

Chapter 3   31

Tabulation and Analysis of Research

    3.1 Introduction   31

    3.2 Study Population   31

    3.3 Tabulation of Research   32

    3.4 Research Analysis   40

    3.5 Summary Section   45

    3.6 Interview Analysis   47

Chapter 4   49

Theological Reflection: A Biblical Model of Peace, Justice, and Reconciliation

    4.1 Biblical Understanding of Peace   49

    4.2 Biblical View of Justice   52

    4.3 Biblical View of Reconciliation   54

Chapter 5   57

Summary and Analysis of the Findings and Search for the Way Forward

    5.1 Introduction   57

    5.2 The Implications of the War   58

    5.3 People's Views of the Peace Talks and Agreement   61

    5.4 The Six Protocols: An Overview   62

    5.5 Methods of Forgiveness   65

        5.5.1 Unconditional Forgiveness of Perpetrators of Crimes   65

        5.5.2 Forgiveness with Justice   67

        5.5.3 Forgiveness and Compensation   69

    5.6 The Role of the Church in Reconciliation and Peace   71

    5.7 The Role of the Government   72

        5.7.1 The Role of the Government of South Sudan in Reconciliation and Peace   72

        5.7.2 Separation of South Sudan from the North   73

Chapter 6   75
    Summary Conclusions and Recommendations
        6.1 Summary Conclusions   75
        6.2 Recommendations   77
           6.2.1 Recommendations for the Church   77
           6.2.2 Recommendations for the Government   78
        6.3 Areas for Further Research: 80

Appendix   81

Bibliography   87

Acknowledgements

I will start my acknowledgement with my boss Rev. Canon Dr. Oliver Meru Duku, Principal, Bishop Allison Theological College, who on behalf of the College dedicated himself to find a scholarship and granted for me a study leave. To him and the college, I say a big thank you.

Thanks a great deal to CMS London for granting me a scholarship without which I would not have been able to study.

The library staff at Uganda Christian University, staff of the New Sudan Council of Churches Resource Centre (Reconcile), Kampala, and those at the World Bank Resource Centre-Kampala, my research assistant and Uncle Robert Malish of the New Sudan Centre for Documentation and Statistics-Yei County, the respondents, interviewees and all who assisted my in collection of the data used in this writing, I am indebted to them all.

I couldn't have managed to complete this dissertation without the encouragement of my dear wife Alidri Faith Grace, who always kept on encouraging me not to worry and assuring me that I would complete the work in time. This gave me courage and assurance I needed so badly. To her I give special thanks.

I am most grateful to my supervisor, Rev. Daniel Button who very often assured me of my capability to finish this work. He politely assisted me in the organization and writing of the dissertation. I thank God for the time I spent with him to produce this work and pray that it will be used for his glory.

Abstract

This research is about the Christian perspective of reconciliation and peace in South Sudan. Sudan was a country gripped in what was set to be, until recently, Africa's longest running civil war. Since its creation, the Sudanese state had been, on many occasions, inherently unjust, repressive, and extremely violent against sections of its own citizens. That was why segments of its people had taken up arms against it.

There were diverse roots of the conflict, which stretch deep into the history and geography of the country. Besides the major civil war, continuous tribal conflict had been experienced among the tribes in the South. This led to the breakdown of interrelationships among the communities in South Sudan. There is a widespread feeling of hate and revenge, biding for the first opportunity to explode. Now that the Comprehensive Peace Agreement has been signed, it is feared there is a strong hope of settling accounts which will threaten the agreement.

This study sets out to investigate people's views and trends to find out whether the end of hostilities would mark the end of interpersonal, group, tribal, and interethnic conflict created by the war. It asks, are people ready to forgive those who could have wronged them during the war without demanding for justice? Is the Comprehensive Peace Agreement valuable and genuine? What would constitute true peace in Sudan? Do the church and the government in Sudan each have a role in bringing sustainable peace?

Field research was carried out using interviews and a questionnaire from high school and college students, church and community leaders, and civil servants. These men and women were between twenty-five and eighty-four years old from fourteen tribes of South Sudan.

The tabulated and analyzed results showed that all people supported the need for reconciliation and peace but proposed different methods of conducting it: unconditional forgiveness with justice and forgiveness with compensation.

The Peace Agreement was considered valuable and genuine because it addressed the root causes of the conflict and because it had both international and regional guarantees. People argued that if it could be implemented, it would give prospect of lasting peace in the country.

To constitute true peace in South Sudan there is need for equality and justice, observation of the law, democratic governance, complete transformation, equitable distribution of resources and services, and freedom of worship.

Furthermore, the findings acknowledged that both the church and the government have a big challenge and critical role to play if sustainable peace is to be achieved.

The general conclusion is that memories of the war are still fresh in people's minds. But it is timely to talk about reconciliation because it is a journey and it entails time. The government should recognize the trauma people had gone through, deal with the root causes of the conflict, and also address the crimes committed during the war so that the wounds inflicted can be healed for people to live harmoniously with one another. For forgiveness to have real meaning there must be full and honest accounting of the facts and confession of crimes and wrong doings committed during the war. The church should teach the people the biblical understanding of peace and reconciliation: that repentance and forgiveness are necessary to the process of reconciliation. The church has to encourage the good traditional conflict resolution and reconciliation techniques.

CHAPTER 1

Introduction

1.1 Background to the Study

This study is about Sudan, a country whose culture has been full of oppression, injustice, war, and violence which undermine human underpinnings of peace and justice. The previous history of the country, both pre-colonial and colonial, is a widely recognized major factor in the political turbulence in the country. Violence characterized much of the nineteenth century, such that even when the British colonialists imposed peace on the country, South Sudan was left disastrously unprepared for political independence. This was worsened by the competition for scarce resources such as labor, good agricultural and grazing land, the Nile waters, and, in the last century, oil. But religion has also been one of the factors of the conflict.[1]

The current conflict in Sudan started in August 1955 shortly before independence, but its roots stretch deep into the history and geography of the country.[2] With bitter experiences from such a long period of war, many South Sudanese think the only way of solving their problems is through revenge and violence. For this reason the church has a great role to play in the process of reconciliation and peace. This responsibility is not limited to ensuring the signing of a peace agreement but extends beyond it, because many wars have been ended with cessation of hostilities but without

---

1. Yusuf Fadl Hasan and Richard Gray, eds., *Religion and Conflict in Sudan. Papers from an International Conference at Yale* (Nairobi: Pauline Publications, 2002), 10.
2. Fadal and Gray, *Religion and Conflict in Sudan*, 13.

attaining true or lasting peace. This is because peace is not just the cessation of hostilities or absence of war as will be explained in the following sections of this thesis. As such, the church can be a reconciling agent by educating individuals and communities about the evils of conflict. It should emphasise that reconciliation, peace, and justice are essential elements of social reconciliation in a conflict situation.[3]

The Sudanese people have passed through tumultuous events in this period of war. There has been terrible human suffering often inflicted as much by rival rebel groups as by government troops and security agents. The war has had a negative impact on the social and spiritual fabric of society. There has been destruction of churches; confiscation of church property; displacement and torture of people; looting; rape; abductions of men, women, and children; ethnic cleansing; destruction of property; slavery and slave trade; abuse of human rights; racial discrimination; burning of villages; forced displacement; killing; and isolation of whole communities.[4] This has left the survivors with great bitterness, hatred, and the spirit of revenge. Ending the military conflict alone will not bring true peace and harmony.

By signing the Comprehensive Peace Agreement between the government of Sudan (GOS) and the Sudan People's Liberation Movement/Army (SPLM/A) there will be an inevitable end to the war which ravaged Sudan for twenty-one years. It can be very easy to start a war because one needs very little effort to do that. But the most difficult thing is to put an end to it. The longer the war continues the more complicated it becomes, and therefore the more difficult it becomes to remember what has become entangled during the period of war. To solve the Sudanese problem comprehensively, one must not therefore forget the marginalized areas, the militias,

3. Simon Fisher et al., eds., *Working with Conflict. Strategies for Action: Responding to Conflict* (UK: ZED Books, 2000), 125.
4. International Crisis Group, *God, Oil & Country: Changing the Logic of War In Sudan. ICG Report No. 39* (Brussels: International Crisis Group Press, 2002), 106, 108, 116–117, 121–122, 124, 136; and Mary Anne Fitzegerald, *Throwing The Stick Forward: The Impact of War on Southern Sudan Women. African Women for Peace Series* (Nairobi: United Nations Development Fund for Women (UNIFEM), 2002), 78; and John Prendergast and Nancy Hopkins, *For Four Years I Have No Rest: Greed and Holy War in the Nuba Mountains of Sudan. Horn of Africa Discussion Paper Series. Paper No. 5* (Washington: Centre of Concern, October, 1994), 30.

the internally displaced people, the refugees, the disabled combatants, the child soldiers, the orphans, the widows, the aged, the rape victims, the looted, the mistreated, etc. In suggesting a solution to these many problems the researcher is not referring to the nature of the agreement between the Sudanese government and the SPLM/A. But the researcher is looking at the problem on a smaller scale, at the level of the individual and the communities. Those dislocated by the internally displaced people will want to know what they must do to drive away somebody's cattle from eating their crops. The widow would want to know whether the killers of her husband will be brought to any justice. The husband or the parent who was ordered to witness the rape of his wife or daughter would be asking whether justice would be brought to bear on the perpetrators. The church's appeal to people to forgive might receive a retort: should confession and repentance not precede forgiveness as the word of God says in the Bible (1 Jn. 8–9). How can the perpetrators be brought to confess and repent of their deeds so that they can genuinely be forgiven? Perhaps in a manner similar to that of the South Africa Truth and Reconciliation Commission?[5]

The South African Truth and Reconciliation Commission (TRC) was set up by the Government of National Unity to deal with what happened under apartheid. The conflict during this period resulted in violence and human rights abuses from all sides. No section of society escaped these abuses. To promote unity and reconciliation, a commission is a necessary exercise to enable people to come to terms with their past on a normally accepted basis and to advance a course of reconciliation. The TRC has three committees: the Amnesty Committee, the Reparation and Rehabilitation Committee, and the Human Rights Violations Committee.[6]

The church, as the strongest community network at the grassroots level, has to take the initiative to bring reconciliation among individuals and between communities. It should mobilize the people to become agents of

5. Clement Janda. "The Challenge of Christian Ministry in Post-war Sudan." An Address at the Third Graduation Ceremony of Bishop Allison Theological College, Arua on March 27th 2003.
6. *The Road to Reconciliation* (2001), available at: http://www.doj.gov.za/trc/legal/act9534.htm. Accessed on 20th February 2005.

reconciliation and healing in their communities. However, the church has to ensure that peace is to be sustained by:

1. ensuring justice;[7]
2. building and sustaining true reconciliation; and
3. bringing institutions to protect human rights.

The work of building peace, which has evaded the Sudanese for so long, is a major challenge for both the church and the government of Sudan. The church has to display Christ's power for forgiveness, for healing, and for transformation. It should lead in educating people and mobilizing the communities for peace. Much needs to be done to bring reconciliation and forgiveness among the people. People should be able to look at their mistakes and say, "I am sorry!" Christians need to clean their house first so that they can be better agents of healing for their country.

History reveals that wars seldom solve problems. Far more often they simply create new problems. Post conflict resolution is one of the great challenges of the modern age. After the chaos and tragedy of the long war in Sudan, the problems will by no means be over even as the peace agreement is signed. Numerous internal wrangles will develop. Pressures and ensuing pain are destined to be intense. It is likely to be a very trying, tedious, and possibly even dangerous period. Instead of peace there will likely be heightened interpersonal, intertribal, and interethnic conflict among the South Sudanese tribal groups ignited by the atrocities committed during the war.

Therefore, for cohesive and peaceful existence, this research will show that the church is the only institution which can bring dramatic transformation in this situation. It can do this not by pointing fingers at the perpetrators of the atrocities and injustices nor granting blanket amnesty to them, but by helping them to acknowledge the unparalleled destruction and pain they inflicted on their victims and to seek for forgiveness and renewal. The church in South Sudan has a more important campaign than the government—which has former-opposing combatants—of building true peace based on reconciliation and justice.

7. In such a complex and long term multiple tied conflict justice means giving people their due by making reparations and punishing human rights violators where necessary.

1.2 Statement of Problem and Definition of Terms

1.2.1 Statement of the Problem

Although a peace agreement between the GOS and the SPLM/A has been signed in Nairobi, Kenya to end twenty-one years of civil war in Sudan, there are some serious unresolved problems and underlying conflicts which have not been addressed and cannot be resolved by the Comprehensive Peace Agreement alone.

1.2.2 Definition of Terms

Peace is not just the end of war, but it signifies salvation, wholeness, integrity, community, righteousness, justice, and well being. It implies right relationship with God, fellow humans, and God's created order.[8] *Reconciliation*, which is a renewal of warmth and trust after a period of hostility and conflict aimed at healing and related to forgiveness,[9] is part of peace. *Justice* is rendering to people what is due them or treating people fairly.[10]

These concepts are explored deeper in chapter 4.

1.3 Hypothesis

The search for true peace in South Sudan, following the end of hostilities, does not end in reconciliation alone but in the combination of peace, reconciliation, and justice. A peace treaty may not represent peace at the local level and therefore may not reach issues of reconciliation, peace, and justice. The church may be the only institution which can effectively bring about a true and lasting peace at this local level.

---

8. David Atkinson and David H. Field, eds., *New Dictionary of Christian Ethics and Pastoral Theology* (England: IVP, 1995), 655.
9. Atkinson and Field, *New Dictionary of Christian Ethics and Pastoral Theology*, 725.
10. James Macquarrie and James Childress, eds., *A New Dictionary of Christian Ethics* (London: IVP, 1986), 330, 331.

1.4 Justification of the Study

The researcher seeks to ensure peaceful and reconciled communities in South Sudan for the service of God and development of the country.

Sudan is one of the countries in the Horn of Africa's complex and conflict-ridden area of the world. The church has to be helped to brace itself for the transition process from conflict situations to peace in order to curb the dangers that might persist long after the formal ending of the conflict. Reconciliation and peace is a matter of crucial significance for the existence of both the church and Sudan as a nation, given the tragic history of interethnic conflict in the country during the period of war. Sudan surely needs healing and reconciliation. The greatest challenge facing the church and the state in post war Sudan will be how to bring reconciliation and healing to those involved in the innumerable atrocities committed by Sudanese upon Sudanese during the war.

Even with a full peace agreement now in place, peace will be very fragile. Much work will be required to ensure the continuation of peace as the Sudanese people work to heal and rebuild the communities.

As peace for Sudan is about to be reached, unusual stories are beginning to emerge in South Sudan which suggest that the victims of the atrocities committed during the war have started sharpening their machetes in preparation for revenge on the perpetrators of these atrocities. Such atrocities include ethnic cleansing, bombing of civilians, arbitrary arrests, lynching, political murders, disappearance of political activists and detainees, rape, looting, genocide, etc.[11]

In order not to plunge into the cycle of violence, there is need for a peace that is just, practical, and one that will actually work and can be implemented. This is not a kind of peace that is only on paper, but one that can resolve issues and change people's lives on the ground and put an end to the twenty-one years of civil war.

---

11. Victor Lugala, *"Reconciliation: A Case for S. Africa Model."* The Sudan Mirror: For Truth and Justice Vol. 1 Issue No 16. Monday December 15th to Sunday December 28th 2003: 10.

The church has the potential to bring about a new hope for the people of Sudan because its leaders have been with the people throughout the long years of war; hence, they know what their people have experienced and command their respect.

Sudan's future political coherence demands reconciliation, peace, and justice as the only way toward reconciling Sudanese individuals, cultures, and religious groups. It is only until the Sudanese begin to listen, learn to repent, and forgive one another that an essential process of building a cohesive society will begin, and only then will true peace be restored. This means that the kind of country Sudan will be, now that a peace agreement is finally signed, is dependent on how reconciled its people are going to be.

It is the hope of the researcher that this research will contribute toward the process of finding a just and true peace; and in particular to determine ways in which the church might effectively lend its efforts to the crucial areas of forgiveness, reconciliation, justice, and ultimate healing.

1.5 Significance of the Study

- This thesis aims to help break the barriers created during the war and make diverse people one in Christ.
- It hopes to prepare the church for its role in public witness in post conflict South Sudan and offer a message of reconciliation and peace.
- It seeks to ensure reconciled and peaceful coexistence of South Sudanese communities.

1.6 Specific Immediate Objectives

- To discover the feelings that people currently have now that a peace agreement has been signed.
- To find a way to move from the South Sudanese's current understanding of peace to the biblical view of peace.

- To find the most effective ways for the church to aid in this process.

1.7 The Scope of the Study

This study is based on reconciliation and peace in South Sudan but more specifically in the diocese of Yei in the Episcopal Church of Sudan and Arua in Uganda. Yei has been chosen because it is well known by and accessible to the researcher. Furthermore, Yei has various tribes of South Sudan, while Arua has many Sudanese refugees.

Therefore, the study covers various views of South Sudanese and is fairly a good sample for the research. The study covers the period from 1983 to early 2005. This was the period of the war. However, it is not a comprehensive study of what happened during this period, rather it seeks to find out people's views on the effects of the war on them personally and on their communities and whether they are ready to forgive those who have wronged them.

1.8 Methodology

The method used in this research is non-literary based. Data primarily came from social research drawn from questionnaires and key informant interviews. But literature is used indirectly to assist with theological formulation and history of the conflict.

Data collection took place between September 2004 and early January 2005. Permission to conduct the research was sought for and granted by the office of Sudan Relief and Rehabilitation Commission (SRRC) in Yei.

Oral Interviews
Selected intellectuals, SPLM/A representatives, youths, church, and cultural leaders were interviewed and notes taken by the researcher to get direct information from both literate and illiterate persons. These particular

groups of people were chosen because they are knowledgeable of the issues under study. The researcher interviewed forty-five people: males and females between twenty-five and eighty-four years old. This is the age of the adult population. They included high school and college students, church and community leaders, and civil servants because they have key perspectives in society. The interview was conducted on the traditional methods of reconciliation and peace making among South Sudan communities whose members were interviewed. Some of those interviewed were also given the questionnaires because they were resourceful in both aspects of data collection.

Questionnaires

One hundred and twenty questionnaire papers were designed and distributed to respondents to be filled. The questionnaire was distributed to officials in various departments. For example, accountants, administrators, magistrates, teachers, and police officers, among others. As such, only one research assistant was required to assist in distributing the questionnaire, while the researcher for accuracy carried out interviews. The questionnaires were administered for a period of four months. Eighty-two answered questionnaires were received. The researcher's target was to have eighty, (as a two-thirds response will still represent a valid cross-section of representatives) because the research was conducted before the Comprehensive Peace Agreement was signed and other areas were not accessible. Through the questionnaire, it was possible to reach those who were not easily accessible for interviews.

Secondary Sources

Because the process is still unfolding, there is no literature yet available dealing directly with the conflict areas at the community level. However, written sources on reconciliation, peace, and justice were searched. This enabled the researcher to get a broaden perspective on the conflict through secondary sources so as to gain indirect assistance on peace building. The sources searched included the following categories:

1. news articles (1997–2005)

2. Internet
3. reference books

A complete list of these sources can be found in the bibliography.

1.9 Limitations

There was lack of adequate documentation as the research dealt with an ongoing conflict. However, the researcher partially overcame this problem by using information on the Internet and newspaper reports.

It is difficult to undertake any kind of study in Sudan today due to the ongoing war in the country. There are suspicions of spying by the security agents. This makes it difficult to access all the vital information one needs. This limitation was overcome by approaching the local authorities to grant the researcher permission to carry out the research. The researcher also had to give more questionnaires than needed knowing that some might not be returned for the reason stated above. Twenty-five percent of the necessary eighty percent were late. The researcher had to persistently follow up in order to get them back.

Difficulties in movement due to poor a transportation system and limited financial resources made it difficult to go to other parts of South Sudan. This limitation was overcome by giving the questionnaire to and interviewing Sudanese refugees in Arua.

1.10 Literature Review

1.10.1 Socio-Political Reconciliation and Peace

In his forward to David Shenk's book *Justice, Reconciliation and Peace in Africa*, John Mbiti, an African writer, said justice, reconciliation, and peace are extremely important concerns. Their theme is as old as the human race itself. That wherever people are found, the sinful elements of strife, conflicts, dissension, and war surface in one form or another. In such a case, therefore, justice, reconciliation, and peace are necessary in order to overcome these destroyers of human society. Furthermore, God desires peace and is pre-eminently concerned about justice, reconciliation, and peace among his people.[12]

According to Dr Villa-Vicencio in *Life and Peace Institute, Horn of Africa Programme Workshop Report*, political reconciliation does not necessarily include forgiveness: reconciling post-conflict nations can settle for less than forgiveness, which is not a priority in nation building. It is not a political task of the state. Forgiveness demands more than statecraft can deliver. The state can, however, create a context conducive to reconciliation enabling people to learn to live together in pursuit of the common good. Political reconciliation is a serious option for living together in the midst of unresolved conflict. It does not imply the resolution of prevailing conflicts or necessarily the solving of the problems involved. It involves the establishment of a relationship, which enables former enemies and antagonists to address prevailing problems in a viable and co-operative manner. In societies emerging from violent conflict, political reconciliation is often the only realistic alternative to enduring and escalating violence.[13]

According to Nat J. Collete, et al., in *The Transition from War to Peace in Sub Saharan Africa*, the most desired outcome for a country and its people should be prevention of conflict. Where conflict has occurred, the work of reconciliation has to be done. Reconciliation means bringing people to have faith again in the civil institutions, in justice, and in the rule of law. In the final analysis, lasting reconciliation must be built on forgiveness.[14] Collete and Michelle L. Cullen in *Violent Conflict and the Transformation of Social Capital* further say that although a peace agreement has been signed to end war in a country, the country has to make great strides toward reconciling its people for sustainable peace, growth, and development. Justice toward those responsible for crimes during the war should be carried out. Priority should be given to reconciliation and peace building to curb ethnic

---

12. David W. Shenk, *Justice, Reconciliation and Peace in Africa. Revised Edition* (Nairobi: Uzima Press, 1997), vi, vii.
13. Life and Peace, 43.
14. Nat J. Colleta et al., *The Transition from War to Peace in Sub Saharan Africa* (Washington DC: The International Bank for Reconstruction and Development/ The World Bank,1996), 75.

and tribal feuds so as to create meaningful relations among individuals and communities. The solutions to conflict prevention lie not only in demilitarization and jump starting the economy but also in good governance—the rule of law, justice, and human rights—and in strengthening social capital at every level.[15] A more secure foundation of a nation which has just emerged from war and violence is reconciliation and peace. Hence the role of the church and government in the promotion of reconciliation and peace is enormous and precarious. It is the duty of the church, the government, and civil society to make the country a better and just place for all to live harmoniously. The key to this lies in the reorientation of the people's minds to construct a democratic, peaceful, and just society.

John Galtung in *Promoting Justice and Peace through Reconciliation* defines justice as to each party a due and describes peace as a capacity to handle conflict non-violently and creatively. That peace requires the components of justice, parity, equality, and equity to work in unison. That reconciliation emerges after a conflict as the parties involved undergo a process of healing and closure.[16]

Walter Wink in *Healing a Nation's Wounds. Reconciliation: A Road to Democracy*, contends that one of the most delicate issues involving reconciliation is what one does with the human right violators after liberation is achieved. He wonders whether they should be given blanket amnesty, given immunity from prosecution, or allowed to continue holding positions in the police or armed forces and treated as if they were acting in the line of duty. Wink argues that amnesty should not be given until all the facts are out and the victims have had their say. That amnesty should be the last step in the process of reconciliation.[17]

---

15. Nat J. Collete and Michelle L. Cullen, *Violent Conflict and the Transformation of Social Capital: Lessons from Cambodia, Rwanda, Guatemala and Somalia. Conflict Prevention and Post Conflict Reconstruction* (Washington DC: The International Bank for Reconstruction and Development/ The World Bank, 2000), 98, 122.

16. American University. *Promoting Justice and Peace through Reconciliation*: (1990). Available at http/:www.American edu/academic.depts/acainst/cgy/reconciliation.htmand coexistance alternatives –conferenc-summary=American University. Accessed on 20th January 2006.

17. Walter Wink, *Healing a Nation's Wounds. Reconciliation: The Road to Democracy* (Sweden: Life and Peace Institute, 1997), 29.

1.10.2 Biblical Reconciliation and Peace

The previous is different from biblical or religious reconciliation which involves forgiveness and full-scale unity (2 Cor 5:11ff; Eph 2:11). God has brought people back to himself by blotting out their sins and making them righteous, and so they have the privilege of encouraging others to do the same. They have the ministry of reconciliation. They are sent with Christ's message of reconciliation to the world. Biblical reconciliation has everything to do with wholesome self-identity; with close relationships to God, neighbor, and community. Ephesians adds one component that, before Christ's coming, Gentiles and Jews kept apart from one another. Jews considered Gentiles beyond God's power and therefore without hope. Christ revealed the total sinfulness of both Jews and Gentiles, and then he offered salvation to both. Only Christ breaks down the walls of prejudice and reconciles all believers to God.[18]

Russ Parker in *Healing Wounded History: Reconciling Peoples and Healing Places* says that Godly reconciliation does not settle for an uneasy peace where the parties in dispute find ways to coexist. The Christian understanding of reconciliation according to Parker is to bring healing of relationships through God's grace in Christ.[19]

According to Laurenti Magesa and Zablon Nthamburi in *Democracy and Reconciliation: A Challenge for African Christianity*, in reconciliation, no person or persons should be seen as inferior, but all should be regarded as equal human beings. When seen in this perspective, people can ultimately reconcile. Magesa and Nthamburi say that there is no possibility of reconciliation among people in conflict until the oppressive structures and institutions are transformed. True reconciliation does not allow the sin of injustice and oppression for this would be a false peace and counterfeit reconciliation.[20]

---

18. *Life Application Study Bible. New International Version* (Michigan: Tyndale House Publishers, Inc., 1991.
19. Russ Parker, *Healing Wounded History: Reconciling Peoples and Healing Places* (London: Darton, Longman and Todd Ltd, 2002), 81.
20. Laurenti Magesa and Zablon Nthamburi, ed., *Democracy and Reconciliation: A Challenge for African Christianity* (Nairobi: Acton Publishers, 1999), 220.

Forgiveness is central to reconciliation and is freely given but not cheaply received. There are conditions for one to receive its full benefits and this involves confession, repentance, and acceptance. The victim-savior offers unconditional forgiveness to all that will believe and accept. That offer is unconditional, but for the oppressor to benefit from it, repentance becomes a condition. The real starting point of reconciliation is willingness to reflect, listen, and understand the situation from various perspectives. The church is an instrument of God's reconciliation. Christians are forgiven people, learning to forgive as God in Christ has forgiven them. The model of forgiveness for the Christian is patterned after Christ's forgiveness.[21]

There is an urgent need for the church to take a vigorous role in civic education and strengthening civil society for transformation of society. It needs to rise to the challenge of ministering healing to the traumatised Sudanese people.

1.10.3 Reconciliation and Peace in South Sudan Context

It is very difficult to find any contemporary literature on South Sudan. However, a journal of New Sudan Council of Churches published in 2002 has an article dealing with the People-to-People Peace Initiative which sheds a new life on the process described in this paper.

The churches in South Sudan, in *Inside Sudan: The Story of People-to-People Peacemaking in Southern Sudan*, were unable to meet the challenge of ending the killing, stopping the war, and seeking justice for their peoples. In order to meet this challenge, the New Sudan Council of Churches (NSCC) came up with what it calls a People-to-People Peacemaking process. The People-to-People Peacemaking process has made significant strides in bringing reconciliation and peace among communities who have been in conflict and war for many years.[22]

---

21. Life and Peace Institute, Horn of Africa Programme. Workshop Report. Sudan Church Leaders' Peace Building and Civic Education held at Jinja Nile Resort—Uganda, August 4–15, 2003, 50, 51.
22. New Sudan Council of Churches, *Inside Sudan: The Story of People-to-People Peacemaking in Southern Sudan. A Peace of the People by the People for the People* (Nairobi: NSCC, 2002), 10.

Warring tribes agreed peace among their communities and seal agreements with a traditional ceremony of cutting the tip off a goat's ear, testing
the blood, and swearing that "Like this ear, God will cut out whoever kills
our peace!" Agreements such as this enabled the Dinka and Nuer to share
pastures and fishing grounds, guaranteed safe passage through respective
territories, training teachers, opening schools, and co-operating in others
ways to rebuild their communities. Similar agreements were reached between different tribes, clans, and communities.[23]

The basis of the People-to-People Peacemaking process is the theory
that since peace would be agreed on and determined by the people, they
would be more likely to keep and enforce the peace. The ideas used in this
approach are rooted in traditional conflict resolution among Sudanese as
well as modern techniques and have evolved into New Sudan Council of
Churches' People-to-People Peacemaking process. These peace conferences
were founded as grassroots movement in peace and have remained as such
to this core premise ever since. The New Sudan Council of Churches has
facilitated various peace meetings among South Sudanese tribes and communities. These include New Sudan Council of Churches's Lokichoggio
meeting for tribal leaders, the Dinka and Nuer Chiefs' and selected church
leaders' meeting and the Wunlit Peace Conference.[24] Most significant of
these was the Wunlit conference between the Dinka and Nuer. It was at-
tended by over one thousand participants who included members of tribes
and communities that had been involved in a bitter conflict for more than
a decade. They had killed one another on battle fields and burned one
another's homes to the ground. That is the past. But everyone gathered
longed to forgive the past and sing in hope of a peaceful future. They had
come with a commitment to agree that it was time to make peace; that they
are determined to have reconciliation between the tribes. At the beginning of the conference a white bull (mabior) is slaughtered as a sacrifice of
reconciliation and peace. The elders made peace and took an oath not to
repeat the atrocities previously committed. They placed a curse on anyone

23. New Sudan Council of Churches, *Inside Sudan: The Story of People-to-People*, 48.
24. New Sudan Council of Churches, *Inside Sudan: The Story of People-to-People*, 48.

that partook of the mabior sacrifice and later broke the oath for peace to which they have committed themselves.[25]

According to Monica Kathina in *Dealing with Conflict in Africa*, the New Sudan Council of Churches was encouraged by the success achieved in the West Bank, the People-to-People Peace Initiative focused its program on inter communal conflict in the East Bank in the Bor areas of Upper Nile. Consultations with leaders of various communities saw a breakthrough that led to the Liliir Peace Conference held in May 2000. This meeting endorsed the Wunlit Accord and discussed issues related to animal grazing areas, water points, return of abducted children and women, and declared an amnesty for previous offences against people and property. The meeting ended with a public covenant between all ethnic groups and signing of comprehensive document pledging peace and reconciliation. This accord has been upheld and peace at the community level restored.[26]

These initiatives provide an opportunity to nurture peace from the bottom-up, grassroots, and community levels. Their existence is also an opportunity for the growth of a vibrant civil society, which will play a critical role in supporting a peace process at the grassroots levels. Further, these processes are creating a pool of local knowledge and expertise which interventions can, if well designed, tap into and benefit from.

According to the *Sudan Church Review*, even with a full peace agreement, peace is still very fragile. A lot needs to be done as the Sudanese people work to heal and rebuild their communities. As the strongest community network at the grassroots level, the church has taken the initiative to bring reconciliation among uprooted communities. It is mobilizing the people to become agents of reconciliation and healing in their communities.[27]

According to Samson L. Kwaje in the SPLM/A Press Release, *The Covenant of the People of Southern Sudan: The Process of South-South Dialogue is Launched*, the SPLM/A appealed to all South Sudanese to adopt the spirit of tolerance, forgiveness, and reconciliation. Political parties, religious and

---

25. New Sudan Council of Churches, *Inside Sudan: The Story of People-to-People*, 59, 60.
26. Jane Boulden, ed., *Dealing With Conflict in Africa: The United Nations and Regional Organisations* (New York: Palgrave Macmillan, 2003), 200.
27. *Sudan Church Review: The Review of Sudan Church Association. Autumn, 2004*, 3, 6.

traditional leaders, the warring factions of South Sudan, and the SPLM/A signed an agreement in which they pledge commitment to dialogue towards reconciliation, forgiveness, and unity of the people of South Sudan by which all people and institutions of South Sudan shall be inspired in the discharge of their affairs. The delegates declare and commit themselves and all parties involved to a process of forgiveness, reconciliation, and national healing.[28]

Peace is to be sustained by ensuring justice; by building institutions to protect human rights; by building and sustaining true reconciliation; and by building and sustaining participation in society.

There is an urgent need for the church to take a vigorous role in civic education and strengthening civil society for transformation of society. It needs to rise to the challenge of ministering healing to the traumatized Sudanese people.

The researcher now turns to give the historical, political, religious, and socio-economic factors behind the conflict in Sudan.

---

28. Samson L. Kwaje, *The Covenant of the People of Southern Sudan: The Process of South-South Dialogue is Launched.* SPLM/A Press Release, April 21, 2005.

CHAPTER 2

Background to Sudan's Conflict

2.1 Introduction

To understand the genesis of the war and its impact on the country, it is important to understand the historical, political, religious, and socio-economic set up of the country. This chapter will therefore deal with these aspects respectively.

2.2 Historical Background

Sudan, the largest country in Africa, borders nine countries and has been at war within itself in the years since before independence; that is, seventeen years of the Anyanya War (1955–1972) and twenty-one years of war waged by the SPLM/A from 1983 to 2004. Something must be very wrong, and it is necessary to look deeply into "what went wrong" in order to find solutions to the Sudanese conflict. To do this, it is necessary to present a brief historical background of Sudan and to identify the problems of Sudan.

The present Republic of Sudan got its name from the "Bilaad el-Sud" which in Arabic means "the country of the Blacks." In the Bible times, Sudan was known as "Cush."

In about 450 AD, Christianity entered Northern Sudan and the Christian kingdoms of Nubia, Makuria, Soba, and Alwa flourished for about 1000 years. The Arab Islamic invasion started in about 700 AD, and this was resisted by the Sudanese Christian kingdoms until, when they could not resist anymore, the last kingdoms were superseded by Islamic kingdoms such as the Funj Sultanate in the East and the Islamic Sultanate of Darfur in the West.

The second wave of Islamic expansion in Sudan was in the Turko-Egyptian invasion—mainly military expeditions from 1820. This was a cruel period of inhumanity and slavery when the Turko-Egyptian forces combined with Northern Sudanese Arab slave traders to come to South Sudan for what they called "black gold" (slaves), "white gold" (ivory), and "yellow gold" (gold).

The slave trade continued under the Turko-Egyptian rule to 1881, when an indigenous uprising led by Mohammed Ahmed, who called himself the Mahdi (Messiah) defeated and killed General Gordon and overran Khartoum. The Mahdi State (1881–1897) intensified slave hunting which the civilian population in South Sudan completely decimating whole tribes.

The rampant slave trade in Sudan and the humiliation, defeat, and death of General Gordon compelled the British and the Egyptians to send a combined force, under Lord Kitchner, to recapture Sudan. The Mahdist forces were defeated at the end of 1897 and thus was established the Condominium rule, known as the Anglo-Egyptian Sudan (1898–1956), which was really an Egyptian rule.[1]

During the Anglo-Egyptian administration, both North and South Sudan were administered separately as two different entities under the Governor General.

The British introduced the concept of "closed districts" which included South of Nuba Mountains of Southern Kordofan and the Funj areas of Southern Blue Nile. This was intended to close off these areas from the North to protect the indigenous African population and areas from the vagaries of the Arab slave traders and from Islamization and Arabization. The Northern Sudan was ruled as a colonial territory along Islamic and Arab lines with its cultural orientation towards Egypt and the Arab World.

---

1. *The Civil War: Background and Evolution of the SPLM/A* (2004). Official website of the SPLM/A available at: http://www.splmToday.com/modules.php?name=splm&page=peace_docs&sect=1. Viewed on February 25, 2005.

While South Sudan was ruled as a colonial territory where African culture, language, and Christianity were encouraged to flourish to the exclusion of anything Arab or Islamic and with its future orientation towards Africa. Pass permits were required for travel between the North and South. However, in 1947, the British abruptly reversed their policy of "closed districts," and a separate North and South Sudan, and instead decided that the South and North would become one independent country.[2] Some British administrators also harbored the idea that the "African" South should be kept off to become part of East Africa. This stalled much of the progress in the South. The Southerners were largely excluded from development and received few of the economic benefits that the Northern part of the country enjoyed, a trend that pertains even today.[3]

The failure of the Colonial authorities to allow the people of the "closed districts" their right to self determination is one of the main factors that contributed to the civil war in Sudan in 1955–1972. The aim of this war was "independence of South Sudan," and it was led by South Sudan Liberation Movement (SSLM) and its military wing the "Anya Nya" (Snake Poison) guerrilla army. Southerners felt that what happened at independence was mere replacement of one set of masters for another, and of a worse type, and thus the Anya Nya called for full independence of Sudan. This war was successfully resolved by the Addis Ababa Agreement of 1972, mediated by Emperor Haille Selassie of Ethiopia, the All African Conference of Churches (AACC) and sister countries. It is estimated that between 750,000 and 1,500,000 Southerners died in the Anya Nya war.

Although the Addis Ababa Agreement granted South Sudan regional autonomy, after which there was relative peace for 10 years, there was a growing realization by most Southerners that peace would not last. As the North worked to undermine the Addis Ababa Agreement, Southerners prepared for war. The Addis Ababa Agreement failed to satisfy the aspirations of the people of the "closed district." The agreement neither put

---

2. *The Civil War: Background and Evolution of the SPLM/A* (2004). Official website of the SPLM/A available at: http://www.splmToday.com/modules.php?name=splm&page=peace_docs&sect=1. Viewed on February 25, 2005.
3. Fitzgerald, *Throwing the Stick Forward*, 3.

them in the center of power in parity with the North nor did it allow for self-determination. At the same time, the North continued with its project of Islamization and Arabization of the country. President Numeiri started a process of eroding whatever gains the South achieved in the Addis Ababa Agreement and finally abrogated the Agreement altogether in 1982 when he divided the South into three separate mini regions. Worse still, President Numeiri worked to annex the discovered oil fields in the South to the North and proceeded in September of that year to establish Islamic Sharia as the Supreme Law of the Land.

Numeiri's abrogation of the Addis Ababa Agreement, and Southern frustration and dissatisfaction coupled with the increased pace of Islamization and Arabization of the South, led to more hostilities. On May 16, 1983, the Sudanese Army attacked one of its own units of the former guerrillas absorbed in the national army and two battalions in Bor broke away. This led to the formation of the SPLM/A. These units took to the bush and were subsequently joined by students, intellectuals, government officials, and the peasantry. The SPLM/A has been leading the struggle since then to 2005.[4]

Having looked at the historical background, the researcher now turns to the political factors behind the war.

2.3 Political Factors

These factors have to be seen in relation to the historical ones discussed above. It should be noted that "very little activity went on in the South during the Turko-Egyptian, Mahdiyya, and the Anglo-Egyptian regimes," while the North was politically active. The South was administered separately from the North since the beginning of the Condominium rule. The initial aim of the policy was to protect the Southern peoples from the slave trade and put in place some form of government through the chiefs, under the ultimate authority of the British district commissioners. But the

---

4. *The Civil War: Back to the Evolution of the SPLM/A.* Official website of the SPLM/A (2004). Available at: http://www.splmToday.com/modules.php? Accessed on February 25, 2005.

Northerners doubted and feared that the primary aim of the policy was to divide the country. The British had half-hearted, inconsistent, short-sighted, and mostly irreconcilable policies and interests in the South, from which pain and suffering have been the unfortunate consequences.[5]

The British civil secretary who introduced the Southern Policy of "accelerating" the educational and economic development of the South, did not live long enough to see it carried out. He died a few months after the announcement of the policy. His successor "seemed to have already made up his mind that the only option for the South was to join up with the North, not separate." During his tenure of office he held a conference in Juba to "discuss the question of unity between the South and the North." When the conference was convened in June 1947 in Juba, the Northern politicians persuaded the Southerners for unity. While the Civil Secretary argued that the people of the South are inextricably bound to the Middle East or Arabia and Northern Sudan for future development, subsequent events in Sudan that followed this unity meeting proved him and the government he represented terribly wrong. Unity forced on the South became, and still is, an unrealized dream in Sudan of the future, as wars of 1955 to 1972 and 1983 to the present have shown. After considerable discussion and claims of bribery, the Southern delegation agreed to the idea of unity but only with a clumsy promise of safeguards that the Northern delegates detested and regarded as unnecessary, undesirable, and a breach of trust and confidence among brothers. The civil secretary failed to include the safe-guards in his new Southern Policy after the conference, and the Southerners felt betrayed.[6]

Self-determination talks were held in 1953 in Cairo between the Anglo-Egyptian government and the Northern political elite, but the Southern representatives were again left out in this all party agreement in which the question of self-determination for Sudan was decided. This confirmed the Southern fears that the north was out to dominate. When the Southerners asked for a federation or autonomy in parliament, by demanding the

---

5. Isaiah Majok Dau, *Suffering and God: A Theological Reflection on the War in Sudan* (Nairobi: Pauline Publications, 2002), 31, 32.
6. Majok, *Suffering and God*, 33, 34.

question of the South's status solved before independence, they were told "this question would be given full consideration later." However, this promise was not kept and later discovered to be a familiar Northern political gimmick. They threw it out altogether. The South was angry and frustrated as the reality and fear of domination and exploitation stared them in the face.[7]

The Northerners made matters worse for themselves by their negative attitude and behavior towards the Southerners, calling the local people "abiid" or "slaves" or "our slaves," and thus asserting openly that they were the new masters in the South, and they must be obeyed. Resistance was inevitable; war was the ultimate result.

When Sudan became independent on January 1, 1956, a special constitutional committee was set up in September of the same year to prepare a new draft constitution for submission to the new constituent assembly. This committee was to decide the federal concerns of the South as a matter of importance. The committee had forty-three members, of whom only three were from the South. After debating the federal question for a whole year it was finally put to vote in December 1957. But because the majority of the members were from the North, the case for a federal state in the South was rejected.

The North "dreaded opening a floodgate for demands of regionalism from the west and east if the South were granted autonomy or federation." When the military under Ibrahim Abboud took over on November 17, 1958, the parliament was dissolved and Southern dreams of federation or autonomy ceased to exist. The regime's policies toward the South made differences between the South and the North even greater. Its unbridled zeal to spread Islam and Arabic culture in the South as the only way to achieve national unity and harmony alienated Southern people and aroused great fear and consequently stiff resistance. The regime's policies against the South were "based on suppression of the opposition and implementation of harsh measures," which do not take the special condition of the South into consideration. By banning political parties, it deprived the Southern

---

7. Majok, *Suffering and God*, 35, 36.

people of the only forum through which they could voice their grievances. Its expulsion of the foreign Missionaries from the South between 1962 and 1964, accusing them of supporting secessionist aspirations, was a form of religious domination. It further confirmed the Southern fears that "the North was really out to dominate the South not only politically, economically, socially but also religiously and culturally." The real reason behind the forceful expulsion of the Christian missionaries was to make way for a forceful spread of Islam and Arabic culture as shown by the flood of Islamic schools and teachers pouring into the South after the expulsion of the missionaries. Those who dared to oppose these moves were persecuted. The level of terror which ensued forced the Southern population and especially the intellectuals out of the country into exile where they joined the Anya Nya to fight the government.[8]

The military takeover by Jaffer Numeiri on May 25, 1969 put an end to Northern political bickering and paved the way to solving the problem of the South. The military government signed the Addis Ababa Accord in 1972 with the Southern Liberation Movement; an Accord abrogated ten years later by Numeiri himself. The result was the war with the SPLM/A. The main political factors behind the long Sudanese conflict include lingering mutual mistrust and suspicion between the South and North, a well grounded fear of Northern domination, and exploitation which only seemed to be confirmed by successive Northern based government's policies and actions towards the South. Historical Northern suspicion of Southern secessionist intentions aroused by colonial Southern policies and aggravated by persistent Southern calls for special status within the country. There are understandable Southern frustrations and disappointments with the persistent Northern pattern of dishonoring promises. This is reflected by the "safeguards" of 1940s, "full consideration" of the federal question in the 1950s, exclusion in self determination talks in 1953, being ignored in the first Constituent assembly after independence, and the abrogation of the Addis Ababa Accord. Coupled with these are the religious and

---

8. Majok, *Suffering and God*, 37, 38.

socio-economic factors to which the researcher now looks in turns in the proceeding section.

2.4 Religious Factors

The relationship between religion and state is perhaps the most controversial of all the forces driving the conflict in Sudan. The Islamists have dominated the current government since it came to power. This has at times made the divergence between the interests of the government and the secular-minded SPLM/A appear irreconcilable.[9]

The above introduction illustrates that religion plays a major role in South–North relations in Sudan: a country, which is a multi-religious, multi-ethnic, multi-cultural, and multi-linguistic society. This is why efforts to impose uniformity on the Sudanese peoples have created conflict rather than a common identity. The politics, history, and social dynamics of the Sudanese reality and identity, past and present, are deeply rooted in religion. Christianity, Islam, and African traditional religions have considerable following in Sudan which makes the place of religion in the Sudanese politics prominent. This diversity needs compromise not fundamentalism.

Historically, Christianity was introduced to the ancient Sudanese Kingdoms of Maqurra, Alwa, and Dongola in the sixth century. It flourished and became a state religion. Next on the Sudanese religious scene came Islam through peaceful dealings of the Arab traders and settlers who intermarried with the local people. However, the Islamization and Arabization of Northern Sudan gained impetus after 1250 AD. Christianity was finally defeated in 1504 AD, and since then Sudanese Islam acquired a unique Sufi character whose leaders came to represent the embryonic origins of the Sudanese intelligentsia. Their role extended into various aspects of social and political life. Abboud's military regime of 1958–1964 may be regarded as "the most ardent advocate of Arabization and Islamization of the South." Similarly, Numeiri's military regime, especially from 1983–1985, exceeded

---

9. International Crisis Group, *God, Oil and Country*, 93.

that of Abboud in its advocacy of Islamization and Arabization. Numeiri boldly declared the imposition of Sharia Law on the whole country in September 1983, thus widening the gap between the South and the North. This made the place of religion central in the Sudanese political landscape. The current Khartoum Islamic government has open Islamic policies and intentions. Since its coming to power in a coup in 1989, it has "consistently stirred the country towards greater Islamization and Arabization, arguing that this is the wish of the majority who happen to be Muslims." Although they argue that non-Muslims will have equal rights and duties with Muslims regardless of creed, race, culture, and ethnic origin, none of this is anywhere near practical reality as the application of Sharia Law has been at best indiscriminate.[10]

The idea of an Islamic state does not accommodate non-Muslims; their cultures, their religions, their political or civil rights, or their freedoms in any way. No non-Muslim, no matter how qualified he or she may be, can become a head of state in that state. Thus the Islamic state envisaged by the North only aggravates and complicates normal relations between the two regions of the Sudanese nation and renders the chances of national unity remote. The North wants an Islamic state in Sudan, while the South strongly objects to this, opting for a secular state despite the fact that the majority of its people are Christians. Although religion may not be the main factor behind the war in Sudan, if the religious question were solved today other factors may easily follow suit.[11]

The researcher now turns to the last factor, which is socio-economic aspect.

2.5 Socio-economic Factors

There are great socio-economic disparities between the South and the North. The south is "backward and underdeveloped in many ways." There is no proper road system, no standard hospitals, clinics, schools, colleges,

---

10. Majok, *Suffering and God*, 40, 41, 42.
11. Majok, *Suffering and God*, 44, 45.

nor any other important social facilities. In contrast the North is developed and developing at a reasonable rate. It has great agricultural schemes; dams, railways, and reasonably tarmarked roads; a good number of industries, schools, universities, colleges; and many other aspects of socio-economic development. The factors discussed above led to these socio-economic disparities and inequalities.

Trade is also an area in which the South still lags behind. It was and is a monopoly of the Northern traders who operated in the South on permission from the government and shamelessly exploited the local people. Their method of trade included swindling the local people, selling them low quality goods for exorbitant prices, and buying valuable goods from them with counterfeit coins or playing cards. Southern venture into trade has been very slow over the years for many historical, cultural, economic, and political reasons. Since independence, "successive governments in Khartoum did very little to improve economic conditions in the south." They chose to suppress, for political reasons, economic development plans meant to uplift living standards in the South. There has never been any developmental project undertaken in the South since the late 1950s. The South became poorer and was left with no choice but to depend economically on the North making it seriously vulnerable, and it has been exploited time and time again for political reasons. The economic potential of the South was brought to light when rich oil reserves were discovered in the South. But the prospects of building the refineries in the North sparked off violent confrontations between the authorities and the people of the South. This again revived the deeply rooted feelings of suspicion and mistrust in the South–North relations. The inevitable result was a continuation of war. These socio-economic, political, religious, and historical factors have been at the center of the peace talks.[12]

Sudan's long war raged for twenty-one years claiming a terrible toll of death and displacement. While the decades of destruction are too complex to trace back to a single source, several forces propel the war, principally disputes over religion, resources, governance, and self-determination.

---

12. Majok, *Suffering and God*, 46–48.

Concentration of power in a small group of competing elites that has not granted the majority of Sudanese broader economic and political rights has only deepened the country's considerable geographic, religious, cultural, and ethnic divisions. Since independence, little progress has been made in addressing these core disputes. Each of these factors is complicated. In many cases they have interacted to deepen the country's divisions. It is only when some breakthrough is made on these matters as a whole and the government embraces an approach built around genuine power sharing and wealth sharing that the viability of Sudan as a unified state can be guaranteed. Similarly, lasting peace will also be made possible with significant progress in addressing all these issues.[13]

Now the researcher has covered the background of the conflict, the following section will be the tabulation and analysis of the research.

---

13. International Crisis Group, *God, Oil and Country*, xi, 93.

CHAPTER 3

Tabulation and Analysis of Research

3.1 Introduction

This research is based on the current situation and is intended to give a general sense of what people are going through. This chapter tabulates and analyzes the findings of the research to find out people's views and trends on the issues the research set out to investigate.

3.2 Study Population

The study population consisted of the following groups of people:
- High school and college students. These were twenty in number including four female students.
- Civil servants: judges, police officers, teachers and secretaries; non-governmental organizations (NGO) workers and opinion leaders. There were forty-six respondents in the above categories, five of which were women.
- Clergy. There were sixteen church leaders who responded to the questionnaires. Two of them were females.

In all there were eighty-two respondents. The respondents' ages ranged from ninteen to sixty-eight. The lowest educational level was primary school. All except one were Christians.

3.3 Tabulation of Research

Effects of War on Communities and Individuals

THE STUDENT RESPONDENTS

	AGE RANGE		SEX		TOTAL RESPONSES
	19–30	31–59	Female	Male	
Total No. of Respondents	18	2	4	16	20
Shelter	8	2	1	9	10
Food	11	2	3	10	13
Education	15	2	3	14	17
Inability to exploit resources	13	2	2	13	15
Lack of health services	15	2	4	13	17
Lack of clean water	12	2	2	12	14
Poverty	12	2	3	11	14
Disruption of social life	9	2	0	11	11
Lack of transport facilities	11	2	1	12	13
Death	10	2	4	8	12

Table 1:1 – Shows responses of students on the effects of the war.

THE CIVIL SERVANT RESPONDENTS

	AGE RANGE		SEX		TOTAL RESPONSES
	19–30	31–59	Female	Male	
Total No. of Respondents	9	37	5	41	46
Shelter	3	20	2	21	23
Food	5	23	3	25	28
Education	8	34	5	37	42
Inability to exploit resources	4	32	5	31	36
Lack of health services	6	29	5	30	35
Lack of clean water	5	32	5	32	37
Poverty	4	26	5	25	30
Disruption of social life	7	32	5	34	39
Lack of transport facilities	5	28	5	28	33
Death	4	29	5	28	33

Table 1:2 – Shows the responses of the civil servants (who have a role to play in the community) on the effects of the war in the community and in individual's lives.

THE CLERGY RESPONDENTS

	AGE RANGE		SEX		TOTAL RESPONSES
	19–30	31–59	Female	Male	
Total No. of Respondents		16	2	14	16
Shelter		13	2	11	13
Food		13	2	11	13
Education		13	2	11	13
Inability to exploit resources		14	1	13	14
Lack of health services		13	2	11	13
Lack of clean water		14	1	13	14
Poverty		14	1	13	14
Disruption of social life		11	2	9	11
Lack of transport facilities		14	1	13	14
Death		14	2	12	14

Table 1:3 – Shows the responses of the clergy on the above issue. The disproportionate ratio between males and females in this table is because these were the only female clergy in the Diocese of Yei at the time of research.

Atrocities / Human Rights Abuses Committed During the War

THE STUDENT RESPONDENTS

	AGE RANGE		SEX		TOTAL RESPONSES
	19–30	31–59	Female	Male	
Total No. of Respondents	18	2	4	16	20
Looting	13	1	3	11	14
Rape	12	1	3	10	13
Torture	12	1	3	10	13
Killing/Murder	6	2	1	7	8

Table 2:1 – Shows the responses of the student respondents on the atrocities and human rights abuses committed during the war.

THE CIVIL SERVANT RESPONDENTS

	AGE RANGE		SEX		TOTAL RESPONSES
	19–30	31–68	Female	Male	
Total out of 46	9	37	5	41	46
Looting	7	30	5	32	37
Rape	5	29	4	30	34
Torture	7	31	4	34	38
Killing/Murder	3	17	4	16	20

Table 2:2 – Shows the responses of the civil servants on the atrocities or human rights abuses committed during the war.

THE CLERGY RESPONDENTS

	AGE RANGE		SEX		TOTAL RESPONSES
	19–30	31–68	Female	Male	
Total No. of Respondents		16	2	14	16
Looting		15	2	13	15
Rape		14	2	12	14
Torture		13	1	12	13
Killing/Murder		11	1	10	11

Table 2.3 – Shows the clergy's responses to issues of human rights abuses committed during the war.

The Value and the Genuineness of the Comprehensive Peace Agreement

THE STUDENT RESPONDENTS

	AGE RANGE		SEX		TOTAL RESPONSES
	19–30	31–68	Female	Male	
Total No. of Respondents	18	2	4	16	20
Valuable	13	2	3	12	15
Not valuable	4		1	3	4
Genuine	12	2	2	12	14
Not genuine	3		1	2	3

Table 3:1 – Shows the views of the student respondents on the value and genuineness of the Comprehensive Peace Agreement.

THE CIVIL SERVANT RESPONDENTS

	AGE RANGE		SEX		TOTAL RESPONSES
	19–30	31–68	Female	Male	
Total No. of Respondents	9	37	5	41	46
Valuable	7	27	2	32	34
Not valuable	1	9	2	8	10
Genuine	6	26	2	30	32
Not genuine	3	9	2	10	12

Table 3.2 – Shows the views of the civil servant respondents on the value and genuineness of the Comprehensive Peace Agreement.

THE CLERGY RESPONDENTS

	AGE RANGE		SEX		TOTAL RESPONSES
	19–30	31–68	Female	Male	
Total No. of Respondents		16	2	14	16
Valuable		13	2	11	13
Not valuable		3		3	3
Genuine		13	2	11	13
Not genuine		2		2	2

Table 3:3 – Shows the views of the clergy respondents on the value and genuineness of the Comprehensive Peace Agreement.

Treatment of Those Who Perpetrated Injustice During the War

THE STUDENTS' RESPONDENTS

	AGE RANGE		SEX		TOTAL RESPONSES
	19–30	31–68	Female	Male	
Total No. of Respondents	18	2	4	16	20
Forgiveness	14	2	2	14	16
Compensation of victims	3	1		4	4
Forgiveness with justice	9	1	1	9	10

Table 4:1 – Shows the opinions of the student respondents on how the perpetrators of injustice should be treated.

THE CIVIL SERVANT RESPONDENTS

	AGE RANGE		SEX		TOTAL RESPONSES
	19–30	31–68	Female	Male	
Total No. of Respondents	9	37	5	41	46
Forgiveness	4	31	5	30	35
Compensation of victims		7	1	6	7
Forgiveness with justice	4	14	2	16	18

Table 4:2 – Shows the opinions of the civil servant respondents regarding the treatment of the perpetrators of injustice.

THE CLERGY RESPONDENTS

	AGE RANGE		SEX		TOTAL RESPONSES
	19–30	31–68	Female	Male	
Total No. of Respondents		16	2	14	16
Forgiveness		16	1	15	16
Compensation of victims		4		4	4
Forgiveness with justice		7	1	6	7

Table 4.3 – Shows the opinions of the clergy respondents regarding the treatment of perpetrators of injustice

The Role of the Church in the Reconciliation and Peace in South Sudan

THE STUDENT RESPONSES

	AGE RANGE		SEX		TOTAL RESPONSES
	19–30	31–59	Female	Male	
Total No. of Respondents	18	2	4	16	20
Yes	16	2	3	15	18
No					
Activities of Involvement:					
Preaching	15	2	2	15	17
Worships	11	2	2	11	13
Advocacy for peace and justice	17	2	2	17	19

Table 5:1 – Shows the activities the church should be involved in for reconciliation and peace as per the students.

THE CIVIL SERVANT RESPONSES

	AGE RANGE		SEX		TOTAL RESPONSES
	19–30	31–59	Female	Male	
Total No. of Respondents	9	37	5	41	46
Yes	6	37	4	39	43
No					
Activities of Involvement:					
Preaching	6	29	4	31	35
Worships	3	21	1	23	24
Advocacy for peace and justice	5	22	3	24	27

Table 5:2 – Shows the activities of reconciliation and peace for the church's as by the civil servants.

THE CLERGY RESPONSES

	AGE RANGE		SEX		TOTAL RESPONSES
	19–30	31–59	Female	Male	
Total No. of Respondents		16	2	14	16
Yes		16	2	14	16
No					
Activities of Involvement:					
Preaching		13	1	12	13
Worships		11	2	9	11
Advocacy for peace and justice		13	2	11	13

Table 5:3 – Shows the activities of involvement by the church as per the clergy respondents' opinion.

The Role of the Government of South Sudan in Reconciliation and Peace in South Sudan

THE STUDENTS' RESPONDENTS

	AGE RANGE		SEX		TOTAL RESPONSES
	19–30	31–68	Female	Male	
Total No. of Respondents	18	2	4	16	20
Punishment of perpetrators of injustice	8		2	6	8
Granting amnesty to perpetrators of injustice	8			9	9
Setting up Truth and Reconciliation Commission	8	1	1	7	8
Compensating victims of injustice	6			6	6

Table 6:1 – Shows the opinion of the student respondents on the role of the government of South Sudan in reconciliation and peace.

THE CIVIL SERVANTS RESPONDENTS

	AGE RANGE		SEX		TOTAL RESPONSES
	19–30	31–68	Female	Male	
Total No. of Respondents	9	37	5	41	46
Punishment of perpetrators of injustice	5	8	1	12	13
Granting amnesty to perpetrators of injustice	1	26	3	24	27
Setting up Truth and Reconciliation Commission	5	17	2	20	22
Compensating victims of injustice	3	6	1	8	9

Table 6:2 – Shows the role of the government of South Sudan in reconciliation and peace according to the civil servants.

THE CLERGY RESPONDENTS

	AGE RANGE		SEX		TOTAL RESPONSES
	19–30	31–68	Female	Male	
Total No. of Respondents		16	2	14	16
Punishment of perpetrators of injustice		8		8	8
Granting amnesty to perpetrators of injustice		10	2	8	10
Setting up Truth and Reconciliation Commission		10	2	8	10
Compensating victims of injustice		8		8	8

Table 6:3 – Shows the role of the government of South Sudan in reconciliation and peace according to the clergy.

The Constitution of True Peace in South Sudan

THE STUDENT RESPONDENTS

	AGE RANGE		SEX		TOTAL RESPONSES
	19–30	31–68	Female	Male	
Total No. of Respondents	18	2	4	16	20
Separation	10	1	2	9	11
Democratic governance	10	1	1	10	11
Complete transformation	6	1	1	6	7
Justice	18	1	4	15	19
Politics	6	1	1	6	7
Land	5	1	1	5	6
Religion	6	1	1	6	7
Natural resources	7	1	2	6	8

Table 7:1 – Shows the student respondents views on the constitution of true peace in South Sudan.

THE CIVIL SERVANTS RESPONDENTS

	AGE RANGE		SEX		TOTAL RESPONSES
	19–30	31–68	Female	Male	
Total No. of Respondents	9	37	5	41	46
Separation	6	29	3	32	35
Democratic governance	5	25	5	25	30
Complete transformation	2	22		24	24
Justice	7	30	4	33	37
Politics	0	17	2	15	17
Land	0	18	2	16	18
Religion	0	17	2	15	17
Natural resources	0	23	2	21	23

Table 7:2 – Shows the views of the civil servants on the constitution of true peace in South Sudan.

THE CLERGY RESPONDENTS

	AGE RANGE		SEX		TOTAL
	19–30	31–68	Female	Male	RESPONSES
Total No. of Respondents		16	2	14	16
Separation		13	1	12	13
Democratic governance		11	1	10	11
Complete transformation		12	1	11	12
Justice		15	2	13	15
Politics		10	0	10	10
Land		9	1	8	9
Religion		10	1	1	10
Natural Resources		10	1	4	10

Table 7:3 – Shows the views of the clergy on the constitution of true peace in South Sudan.

3.4 Research Analysis

Effects of the War on Communities and Individuals

From the preceding tables 1:1 to 1:3, all categories of respondents identified lack of education as one of the most lacking necessities in South Sudan during the period of the war. This amounts to 72 respondents (88%). This is followed by lack of clean water, health services, and inability to exploit development resources all rated at 65 (79%). Others identified included disruption of social life rated at 64 (78%), death at 59 (72%), poverty at 58 (71%), and lack of transport facilities at 57 (70%). Shelter and food which are basic human necessities were rated at 46 (56%) and at 44 (53%) respectively.

Furthermore, separation of families, insecurity, lack of employment, displacement, being exiled, depopulation, lack of unity among South Sudanese, loss of personal belongings, trauma, collapse of civil society, loss of good social and cultural practices, early pregnancies, and lack of peace and stability were mentioned as some of the things experienced by the communities and individuals during the war.

It was also noted that there are tribal conflicts among South Sudanese, which make them to live in hatred, suspicion, and hostility toward themselves. Some people had been heard as saying that their differences should be given a halt for a while and resume afterward when the civil war is over.

Although these problems were common to the individuals and communities, they seemed not to have affected all individuals at the same rate. For instance, those who got a chance to study or sent their children to school did not regard the education system as being affected by the war. The same applies to the other challenges too. The respondents who were in the urban areas or in exile during the war could probably be the ones who got access to education and other basic services.

Atrocities and Human Rights Abuses Committed During the War

All categories of respondents have responded overwhelmingly to the atrocities or human rights abuses committed against civilians of South Sudan during the war. Tables 2:1 to 2:3 show that the respondents cited looting of property as one of the highest crimes committed. It was rated at 66 (80%). This was followed by torture at 64 (78%), rape at 61 (74%), and killing or murder at 39 (48%). Other abuses include violence against women, women and child abduction, forced marriages, confiscation of people's property, tribalism, defilement, air bombardment, harassment, and destruction of other people's crops by internally displaced people's cattle.

However, as in the above case, there were other respondents who chose a neutral position by not commenting on the subject, while one denied that there was looting, rape, killing, or torture in their community during the war, and yet others rated these atrocities high.

The Value and Genuineness of the Peace Talks and Agreement

While 62 (76%) of the respondents of all the categories regarded the peace talks which led to the signing of the Comprehensive Peace Agreement early this year between the government of Sudan and the SPLM/A as valuable, 17 (21%) respondents regarded the talks not valuable. The remaining 3 respondents were not sure. On the other hand, 59 (72%) of the respondents regarded the same talks as genuine, while 17 (21%) of them were pessimistic and regarded the talks as not genuine. The remaining 6 (7%) took a neutral stand. Some of the respondents seemed not to mind about the valuableness or genuineness of the peace talks so long as these could bring an end to the war in the country. They argued that people are tired of war and urgently need peace. That the peace talks were valuable and genuine not only because they addressed the root causes of the conflict, but also because the Agreement has both regional and international guarantees, which included the United Nations, United States of America (USA), United Kingdom, European Union, African Union, and Intergovernmental Authority on Development. As such the peace agreement is not like former agreements, but it will lead to true peace, development, and independent South Sudan with constitutional rule and respect of human rights. For those in exile the peace agreement will allow them go home.

For others, the peace talks were neither valuable nor genuine because they were not broad based but serve the wishes of the minority and so the peace agreement will collapse. Yet others feel the Southerners were not granted their right, in that the bigger fraction of the oil revenues would have come to the South. While others argued that the Arabs were pressured by the international community, notably the USA to sign the peace agreement. They therefore argued that it is too early to be excited by the agreement; that people should wait to see the government's commitment to implementing it.

Treatment of Those Who Perpetrated Injustice During the War

The respondents showed mixed feelings for the treatment of those who committed atrocities during the war. As shown in tables 4:1 to 4:3, 67 (82%) of the respondents propose that these people be forgiven. However, some 25 (30%) respondents, including some who opted for forgiveness, also argued that the perpetrators could only be forgiven after justice has been done. That is, they have to be prosecuted. The government of South Sudan should set up law courts or a truth and reconciliation commission to deal with such issues. Furthermore, 15 (18%) of the respondents demand compensation as a condition for forgiveness. Others argued that those who committed crimes should repent before they would be forgiven. The elderly people have a more forgiving spirit than the young people who suggested that those who committed atrocities should be executed or sent to exile. While others said that such people should not be assigned public offices. This could have been because on certain occasions the elderly people were respected during the war, but it could also be that the elderly understand what could happen to society when there is no forgiveness.

The Role of the Church in Reconciliation and Peace

In response to the role of the church in reconciliation and peace in South Sudan, all the groups of respondents equally accepted that the church has a great role to play in the process. As shown in tables 5:1 to 5:3, 77 (94%) of the respondents argued that the church can bring reconciliation and peace to South Sudan. The church can do this through its ministry of preaching the message of love, forgiveness, reconciliation, and peace at 65 (79%) respondents, advocating for peace with justice at 59 (72%) respondents, and organising and facilitating reconciliation and peace building workshops at 48 (59%) respondents. The church should also set up counselling centers to counsel people who are affected by the evils committed during the war. It should also engage in conflict resolution to transform people's attitudes and behaviors to create change in the society. The only Muslim respondent further argued that the work of reconciliation and peace building in South Sudan should not be left to the church alone as the Mosques can also play a significant role.

One of the clergy respondents, while recognizing the vital role the church can play at the same time, pointed out that the church can at certain times be impeded from this role because it is not popular with some of the politicians. On the other hand a politician argued that this task is heavily placed on the church because the government will not have the necessary funds to perform it, as the funds available will be used for rebuilding the shattered infrastructure.

The Role of the Government in Reconciliation and Peace

On the role of the government of South Sudan in reconciliation and peace building in the country, as reflected on tables 6:1 to 6:3, 46 (56%) of the respondents recommended that the government grant amnesty to the perpetrators of injustice, while 29 (35%) argued that they should be punished. Furthermore, 40 (48%) of the respondents wanted the government to set up a truth and reconciliation commission to listen to reports and testimonies of victims and call the perpetrators to account. Some of the respondents seemed to hold double views concerning the way perpetrators of injustices should be handled. That is, both punishment and forgiveness. But one of the church leaders cautioned that the situation in South Sudan was that of a civil war and thus unique from that of South Africa under apartheid. In his view, setting up a commission or bringing the perpetrators to account would undermine the leadership of the former rebel leaders who would be placed in high positions of responsibility in the government of South Sudan.

Other respondents argued that the government should address the issues of injustice and govern by rule of law by enforcing law and order: the government should acknowledge the atrocities committed and take people's view on what needs to be done to correct the situation and create a forum to address the issues. Some respondents feared that if perpetrators were given blanket amnesty it would lead to tribal feuds.

For reconciliation and peace, according to other respondents, the government as an institution should treat all its citizens equally and justly. There must be good governance, observation of human rights, and equal employment opportunities to all.

The Constitution of True Peace

Concerning the constitution of true peace in South Sudan as shown in tables 7:1 to 7:3, the respondents identified observation of justice, at 71 (87%), and separation, at 59 (72%), as some of the ingredients of true peace in South Sudan. Others include democratic governance at 52 (63%), complete transformation at 43 (52%), equitable distribution of natural resources at 41 (50%), and freedom of worship at 33 (41%), among others. The students and civil servants respondents regard the issues of separation, justice, and good governance as very important. According to them, if the above issues are properly addressed the others like politics, land distribution, religion, and equitable distribution of natural resources would not be a major problem. Regarding religion, the Muslim respondent argued that freedom of worship is one of the conditions for true peace in South Sudan.

3.5 Summary Section

Effects of War

    Highest level (80–90%)—lack of education

    Medium level (60–79%)—lack of clean water, health services, inability to exploit resources, disruption of social life, death, poverty, and lack of transport facilities

    Lowest level (39–59%)—lack of shelter and food

According to the respondents, education was the most lacking during the war. In spite of food and shelter being basic needs and thus priority according to NGOs, these were rated lowest. Maybe NGOs needed to focus on education.

Human Rights Abuses

    Highest level (80–90%)—looting

    Medium level (60–79%)—torture and rape

    Lowest level (39–59%)—murder

Value and Genuineness of Peace Talks and Agreement

    Highest level (80–90%)

    Medium level (60–79%)—valuable and genuine

    Lowest level (15–59%)—neither valuable nor genuine

That people responded this way suggests they are not sure what the future holds as far as the implementation of the peace agreement is concerned.

Treatment of Perpetrators of Injustice
    Highest level (80–90%)—forgiveness
    Medium level (60–79%)
    Lowest level (15–59%)—forgiveness with justice and compensation

People have mixed views regarding the treatment of those who committed crimes against humanity during the war.

Role of the Church in Reconciliation and Peace
    Highest level (80–90%)—big role to play
    Medium level (60–79%)—preaching and advocacy for peace with
        justice
    Lowest level (39–59%)—workshops on reconciliation and peace

This response suggests how big a role the church is expected to play and thus the need for thorough preparation.

Role of the Government in Reconciliation and Peace
    Highest level (50–56%)—granting amnesty
    Medium level (40–49%)—setting up truth and reconciliation
        commission
    Lowest level (30–39%)—punishing perpetrators

The Constitution of True Peace in South Sudan
    Highest level (80–90%)—rendering of justice and separation of the
        South from the North
    Medium level (60–79%)—democratic governance
    Lowest level (39–59%)—complete transformation, equitable
        distribution of resources, and freedom of worship

3.6 Interview Analysis

The interview was carried out by the researcher among 45 interviewees of both men and women aged between 25 and 84 from 12 tribes of South Sudan. These were SPLM/A representatives, intellectuals, church and cultural leaders, and youths that were well versed with their traditions and cultures.

The interviews were conducted on the traditional methods of reconciliation and peacemaking among South Sudanese communities after fierce conflict. The interview revealed that there were and are varying methods of reconciliation and peace making in many communities. One of the interviewees said "we had our own methods of peace and reconciliation in our community; that was why there were no rampant conflicts."[1]

In the traditional South Sudanese culture, justice and reconciliation took a more meaningful step. Not only were chiefs or community leaders called to judge, but there was also an element of reconciliation. Those who committed serious crimes not only had to be judged but there was an extra rule for one to reconcile with the other party. Sometimes this was done by paying a fine or feeding the parties. This attempt at reconciliation meant the injury suffered by the injured party was no more, and then there was reconciliation between the parties.

The most common response found by this research was that following conflict, the parties involved would live in enmity and not share food until the issue was solved. This was out of fear of infection with leprosy among the tribes in Equatoria. The two parties would gather to discuss the root causes of the conflict, followed by admission of guilt and compensation by the party on the wrong. Where both parties had equally lost, they would either forgive or compensate themselves with animals, foodstuff, or even human beings. For instance, manslaughter among the Dinka was compensated with up to fifteen or twenty-five cows, while murder for between thiry and fifty cows. In some tribes in Equatoria, a young girl or some animals (goats) would be given in compensation in either case. Compensation was

---

1. Ismail Matthew Muktar, Personal interview. October 16, 2004.

to curb unnecessary killings and avoid future conflicts; where compensation failed revenge would occur.

Following compensation, the parties would slaughter an animal and eat together. Elders would warn against re-igniting the conflict. This was a sign of covenant making, reconciliation, peace, and restoration of relationships.

There were some communities which would not ask for compensation for human life because they argued that nothing given would be worth the price of human life. Hence they would cast their grievances to God, the righteous judge. These communities believe that the deceased is alive and "seeing" so he or she would avenge their killer.

Now the researcher turns to the theological reflection or biblical model of peace, justice, and reconciliation.

CHAPTER 4

Theological Reflection: A Biblical Model of Peace, Justice, and Reconciliation

4.1 Biblical Understanding of Peace

In its ordinary usage, "peace" denotes the absence of conflict, violence, war, or strife; the state that obtains between wars, tranquillity. It is philosophy and paradigm with its own values and precepts which provide a framework within which to discern, understand, analyze, and regulate human relationships in order to create an integrated, holistic, and human social order.[1] Biblically, the Hebrew word translated peace is shalom and it abounds in meaning. It refers to salvation, wholeness, integrity, community, righteousness, justice, well being, and harmony that embraces the whole of human life at the level of the individual, family, communities, and nations. Peace in this case, therefore, implies right relationship with God, one's neighbor, and the created order, and is a gift of Christ the beginner of shalom (Eph. 2:18). It is only experienced when people accept God's gift of acceptance and loving forgiveness. This is the peace that God gives and one which the

---

1. Hizkias Assefa and George Wachira (eds.), *Peacemaking and Democratisation in Africa: Theoretical Perspectives and Church Initiatives* (Nairobi/Kampala: East African Educational Pubblishers Ltd, 1996), 42, 44.

world cannot take away (Jn. 14:27).[2] The way of peace consists of values, attitudes, behavior, and methods based on non-violence and respect of the Fundamental Rights and freedoms of every person.[3]

Peace is a desirable end for both individuals and nations. The human heart longs for peace. Peace therefore imposes itself as a primary political objective, which no responsible government can overlook. The prophetic vision of a world in which swords will be beaten into plowshares and spears into pruning hooks (Isa. 2:4b) finds a positive response. Peace, however, has its own condition. Unless fulfilled, the ideal of peace is nothing more than wishful thinking. The main condition for peace is justice (Isa. 32:16, 17). Peace is related to justice as a fruit to the tree that produces it. Where there is no justice, there can be no peace. Injustice and peace cannot coexist. The prophet Isaiah speaks out of a context of injustice and oppression in which the ruling classes have become corrupt and are using their power to exploit the poor (Isa.1:23). Their God-given task is to seek justice, to encourage the oppressed, to defend the cause of the fatherless, and to plead the cause of the widow (cf. Isa. 1:17). Instead, they are busy looking after their own selfish interests (Isa. 5:8). Through unjust laws and oppressive decrees, the poor are deprived of their rights, the widows are exploited, and the fatherless are robbed (Isa. 10:1, 2).

Injustice does not come alone. Where justice is disregarded, anarchy breaks in. The fruit of justice will be peace. Such peace is no mere absence of war, but shalom, that is, harmony, wellbeing, wholeness, abundance, prosperity, health, happiness, and fulfilment both for the individual and for society. It is related to tranquillity; quietness or rest; and confidence, security, or safety. Justice is an essential condition for the existence of shalom. No justice, no peace! Justice and peace are inseparable; they are united in marriage and their marriage is indestructible. In the words of the Psalmist, "love and faithfulness meet together; justice and peace kiss each other" (Psalms 85:10). In the absence of justice only a counterfeit peace

---

2. David J. Atkinson and David H. Field, eds., *New Dictionary of Christian Ethics and Pastoral Theology* (England: IVP, 1995), 655.
3. Simon Fisher et al., eds., *Working with Conflict. Strategies for Action: Responding to Conflict* (UK: ZED Books, 2000), 137.

is possible; the false security of the oppressors, based on coercion, or the slumber of the oppressed, based on fear, but not real, genuine, and lasting peace. While the fruit of justice is peace, the fruit of injustice is violence and social chaos, enmity and insecurity, hatred, and fear. Injustice carries within it the seed of subversion. Justice leads to life; injustice ends in death. Injustice is a sin against the living God, hence those who persist in injustice place themselves under God's judgement.

"He who mocks the poor shows contempt for their Maker; whoever gloats over disaster will not go unpunished" (Prov. 17:5). The most efficient way to work for peace is to work against injustice. "Do you long for peace? Then, let justice roll down like a river, righteousness like a never failing stream!" (Amos 5:24). Do you want "quietness and confidence forever"? Then, "give up your violence and oppression and do what is just and right"(Ezek. 45:9). Do you wish to live "in peaceful dwelling places, in secure homes, in undisturbed places of rest"? Then, this is what God requires of you: "To act justly and to love mercy and to walk humbly before your God" (Mic. 6:8).[4]

In our relationship with God, peace came through Christ's receiving our justice. So in human society it is impossible to have peace where there is injustice. This is also true within a nation: there can be no peace while criminals are at large and where there is injustice. From the biblical perspective, peace is not the absence of war but the restoration of justice in relationships. If people long for peace, their prayers and efforts ought to be devoted to the establishment of justice.[5] In other words, peace requires justice; hence in the transition from war to cessation of hostilities peace, reconciliation, and justice are of paramount importance. Now we turn to justice.

---

4. *Transformation: An International Dialogue on Evangelical Social Ethics. Focus on Central America* (Argentina: January/March 1985/ 86, Vol. 2 No. 1), 2, 3, 4.
5. David R. Clark and Robert V. Rakestraw, eds., *Readings in Christian Ethics. Volume 2: Issues and Applications.* 7th Printing (Grand Rapids, Michigan: Baker Books, 2003), 504.

4.2 Biblical View of Justice

The *English Thesaurus* defines justice as accuracy, equitableness, fairness, honesty, impartiality, justness, and right.[6]

The God of the Old Testament is a God who is passionately concerned about personal ethics and social justice. He is not indifferent to oppression and injustices. God is as burdened about social justice today as he ever was in Amos's day.[7] Justice is that form of moral excellence which demands the righteous distribution of rewards and punishments, and which renders it certain under God's government that obedience will be rewarded and sin punished. It is that perfection of divine nature which renders it necessary that the righteous be rewarded and the wicked punished. The work of Christ is a satisfaction of justice. God cannot pardon sin without a satisfaction to justice. The plan of salvation as unfolded in the New Testament is founded on the assumption that God is just and he is determined to punish sin.[8] But Jesus brought human reconciliation with his heavenly Father through the shedding of his own blood; thus winning for humanity the gift of peace (Eph. 2:14–17).[9]

Justice is a broad biblical principle, which means rendering impartially to everyone his or her due in accord with the right standard of God's moral law revealed in scripture.[10]

Justice is God's communicable attribute, manifesting his holiness. God's relative justice has to do with his rectitude in and of himself; by his absolute justice is meant the rectitude by which he upholds himself against the violations of his holiness. By rectoral justice he institutes righteous just rewards, whereby he metes out rewards (remunerative justice, expressive of his love) and punishments (retributive justice, expressive of his wrath). God's moral excellence made necessary either the punishment of sinners or expiation

6. Children's Leisure Products Ltd, *English Thesaurus* (Scotland: Geddes & Grosset, 2000), 186.
7. Eric S. Fife and Arthur F. Glasser, *Mission in Crisis: Rethinking Missionary Strategy* (London: IVP, 1963), 32, 33.
8. Charles Hodge, *Systematic Theology. Vol. II* (Grand Rapids, Michigan: WM. B. Eerdmans Publishing Company), 290, 291, 292.
9. Robin Gill, *A Textbook of Christian Ethics* (Edinburgh: T&T Clark Ltd., 1989), 277.
10. Clark and Rakestraw, *Readings in Christian Ethics*, 391–393.

whereby their condemnation would be removed. The sinner was without power to offer the satisfaction for his or her sin, but righteousness was provided as Christ, the representative of humanity, met all the righteous demands of the law and paid the price of sin in the believer's place thus meeting the requirements of the divine justice.[11] This makes justice one of the core values and an ingredient of peace and reconciliation.[12]

According to Paul Tillich, there are no conflicts in God between his reconciling love and his retributive justice.[13] He cannot remove the self-destructive consequences of self-existential estrangement because they belong to the structure of being itself and God would cease to be God if he was removed. He would cease to be love, for justice is the structural form of love without which it would be sheer sentimentality. The exercise of justice is the working of God's love, resisting and breaking what is against love. The atoning work of Christ is then construed as the solution that enables God to forgive what has aroused his wrath, because in Christ's death God's wrath is satisfied. The violated justice cannot be re-established by the message of the divine love alone. The message of a divine love, which neglects the message of divine justice, cannot give humanity a good conscience.[14]

The discussion above shows that God is passionately concerned about personal ethics and social justice. Therefore, for one to be at peace with God, one must uphold justice. Peace in this case is not only the absence of violence but also the presence of socio-economic justice whose components are parity, equality, and equity. For this reason, justice is a necessary step on the journey toward reconciliation and true peace. Now the researcher turns to the biblical view of reconciliation.

---

11. Walter A. Elwell, ed., *Evangelical Dictionary of Theology. Baker Books* (UK: Patnoster Press, 1995), 593.
12. Assefa and Wachira, *Peacemaking and Democratisation in Africa*, 66.
13. Paul Tillich, *Systematic Theology. Part III: Existence and the Christ* (London: SCM Press Ltd., 1978), 77.
14. Tillick, *Systematic Theology*, 174, 172.

4.3 Biblical View of Reconciliation

Reconciliation is the renewing of warmth and trust after a period of hostility and conflict. It is making peace between two conflicting individuals, groups, communities, institutions, or nations. Reconciliation is bringing back into fellowship; restoring a right relationship with one's neighbor. Its goal is healing and is achieved when the parties involved in the conflict agree to put behind their differences and make a fresh beginning with each other. Reconciliation is related to forgiveness, which is its important component, yet the two are not identical as forgiveness can be offered in the absence of the person involved in the conflict while reconciliation involves the willingness of both parties to resume the risk of relating to each other once again.[15]

The concept of reconciliation is very important theme in Christian Theology. The term derived its root from the Latin word *conciliatus*, which means "to come together" or "to assemble." It refers to the act by which people who have been apart and split off from one another begin to stroll or march together again. Essentially, it means the restoration of broken relationships or coming together of those who have been alienated and separated from each other by conflict to create community again. Reconciliation is conflict resolution but it has greater dimensions and more profound implications.[16]

There are varied meanings of the word reconciliation used in the Bible. Some of the meanings include a state of national tranquillity, exemption from rage, and havoc of war and peace between individuals. The Bible discusses reconciliation in many contexts from which four dimensions can be discerned: reconciliation with God, reconciliation with the self, reconciliation with neighbors and human community, and reconciliation with nature. For the purpose of this paper the researcher will briefly describe the first and third dimensions. Reconciliation with God means creation of harmony with God by mending the conflicts that separate individuals from God through confession and repentance and request for forgiveness,

---

15. Atkinson and Field, *New Dictionary of Christian Ethics and Pastoral Theology*, 725.
16. Assefa and Wachira, *Peacemaking and Democratisation in Africa*, 46–47.

and a decision to turn away from the misdeeds and rectify them if possible. Moreover, reconciliation with neighbors and the human community at large is transferring to and sharing with other human beings the forgiveness and mercy that the individual has experienced in being reconciled with God.[17]

Theologically, reconciliation follows repentance and pardon. Only then can relationships be built on genuine love and unity. In a Christian's relationship with Christ, the barrier of sin is removed through faith in Christ. The Christian is then reconciled to God, whose holy law is totally satisfied by Christ (Gal. 3:13). Biblically, reconciliation involves paying a price. The atonement is, therefore, the means by which God and man are reconciled to each another. Used in the New Testament passages (Rom. 5:10f; 2 Cor. 5:18–20; Eph. 2:16; Col. 1:20), reconciliation expresses the notion of "making peace" (Rom. 5:1; Col. 1:20).[18] Reconciliation could not be affected without Christ, but its basis is "the death of his Son," " through the Cross," by his bloodshed, "in his body of flesh by his death" (Rom. 5:10; Eph. 2:16; Col. 1:20, 22). God could not ignore the separation made by sin and embrace humanity in fellowship without Christ's death. Humanity was reconciled to God by the death of his Son.[19]

On the basis of this understanding, reconciliation is spelled out more precisely by a closely related term, propitiation, (Rom. 3:25; Heb. 9:5; 1 Jn. 2:2; 4:10), which refers to the removal of wrath by offering a gift. In such offering God was reconciling the world to himself in Christ (2 Cor. 5:19). In forgiveness and reconciliation there is a sacrifice to be made (1 Cor. 5:7; Eph. 5:2; Heb. 7:23; 8:3; 9:23–28; 10:10–26; 13:10–13). This implies that there is no evading of paying the price for reconciliation. It can therefore be argued that reconciliation causes the idea of deliverance by payment of a price to meet God's justice (Ps. 49:7; Isa. 43:3; Mk. 10:45; 1 Pet. 1:18f). There is a theological controversy as to why God should pay price and to

---

17. Assefa and Wachira, *Peace Making and Democratisation in Africa*, 46–59; and *Reconciliation: A TEE Manual For Church Leaders. A Simple Copy for field-testing* (Nairobi: MAP International and NSCC, 2000), 2.
18. Bruce Milne, *Know the Truth: A Handbook of Christian Belief* (England: IVP, 1982), 58, 117, 150, 157.
19. Elwell, *Evangelical Dictionary of Theology*, 917, 918.

whom the price was paid, but these are issues of secondary importance in this paper. What matters is that reconciliation and forgiveness is costly, that was why Christ had to pay the price by his own life.[20]

From the above discussion, we have seen that there is a relationship among reconciliation, peace, and justice. That reconciliation with God is preceded by acts of restitution to satisfy his justice, which in turn are followed by the assurance of pardon and forgiveness. Christ also encourages those who caused injury to others to remove the grievance. The offender has to propitiate or reconcile the offended to himself or herself by whatever compensation may be required (Matt. 5:23–26).

Therefore, people can never talk meaningfully of reconciliation and peace today without considering the issues of justice. Forgiveness is the only path that will build a lasting peace, but it demands that the evil which has been done be acknowledged and corrected. It does not mean giving up on seeking justice, but it enables a person to seek justice and reparation for building a better life. In the context of this study therefore it can be argued that unless basic human rights concerns are seriously addressed it will be difficult to have a lasting peace in Sudan. Hence there is need for justice and reconciliation.

Now the researcher turns to the summary and analysis of the findings and search for the way forward.

---

20. Milne, *Know the Truth*, 157–159.

CHAPTER 5

Summary and Analysis of the Findings and Search for the Way Forward

5.1 Introduction

The conflict in Sudan has been principally about justice: a struggle against injustices and providing justice for all, irrespective of creed, colour, belief, or race. The Sudan government and the SPLM/A signed a historic peace agreement in Nairobi, Kenya on the January 9, 2005 that ended the twenty-one year long war; Africa's longest in Sudan. Some see this as an achievement of justice and equality in Sudan.[1]

This chapter sets out to investigate three major concerns following the signing of the comprehensive Peace Agreement in Sudan. These are the implications of the war; people's readiness for reconciliation without demanding for immediate justice; the people's feelings about the Comprehensive Peace Agreement; and whether there is any role that the church and the government of South Sudan could play to bring about peace and reconciliation. Here the researcher will summarise the results of the findings, and give personal ideas about the situation and a way forward.

---

1. Reuben Olita and Agencies, "Sudan Ends 21-Year War." *The New Vision, Monday, January 10, 2005:1*, 2.

5.2 The Implications of the War

War is an evil activity no matter who wages it and for what objective. Whether brief or protracted, armed conflicts kill and maim people, separate families, and force people from their homes to seek security and survival in refugee and displaced peoples' camps. The situation limits people who otherwise would be self sufficient to depend on others. War also destroys a country's infrastructure and environment. It tears down the social fabric of clan relationships and family bonds for many reasons: death, displacement, hunger, poverty, desperation, selfish motives and anarchy.[2] This is the case with Sudan where million of people have died and others have been displaced in the course of the war, which is over political, religious, and economic domination of the South. The war has disrupted development especially in the South where illiteracy; wanton poverty; disease; hunger and starvation; displacement; cultural, communal and family dislocation; slavery; destitution; the destruction of physical and social environment; hopelessnes; and inhumanity prevail.[3]

Sudan's civil war had been prosecuted with stark brutality, principally by government forces. The government had unleashed indiscriminate aerial attacks, used famine as a weapon of war, forcibly displaced civilians and supported paramilitary forces engaging in slave trade. The SPLM/A and its allied militias had indiscriminately attacked civilian populations, diverted relief supplies, and forcibly recruited soldiers including children. More often the government forces attack civilian targets as part of an effort to weaken support for the insurgents. There were widespread human rights abuses. Although the precise scale of death and destruction resulting from the civil war will never be known, it has been one of the deadliest conflicts since World War II. Much of the human devastation can be traced to the criminal tactics with which the war was fought. Atrocities were routine events. International human rights advocates and lawyers actively debate whether certain practices in Sudan should be characterized as genocide and

---

2. Fitzgerald , *Throwing the Stick Forward*, 85.
3. Michael E. Maragu, Conflict Transformation Manual for South Sudan Peace Building Programme (OXFAM GB South Sudan), 2000.

enslavement or crimes against humanity. Although disagreement is rooted in careful legal phrasing and debate over intent, tactics, culture, and the implications of an official finding of genocide, given the broad body of evidence tactics such as slavery, forced displacement, and using food as a weapon are sufficiently brutal and persistent to qualify as gross violations of international law and of nearly every rule of war applicable to an internal armed conflict.[4]

All parties to the conflict have contributed mayhem that has left the Southern population and people in the marginalized areas most impoverished in the world. The irony is that all this is happening in a country which is one of the world's richest untapped natural resources.[5]

The over two decades of war in Sudan have caused a lot of untold suffering and pain for the people. There has been looting of people's properties, torture, murder, and execution of innocent lives; children and women abductions, amputation and flogging; and interethic, intratribal, intertribal, and interclan conflicts. There has been a lot of insecurity which has resulted in depopulation. Many prominent and innocent people have been lost in the ensuing conflicts. The war has made people vulnerable. They lack shelter since they are constantly displaced. Such displacement has also detached them from their roots resulting in loss of cultural values. There is also lack of food since people, constantly on the move, cannot produce their own food and lack agricultural implements. There is also lack of education and health services, hence there are high rates of illiteracy and mortality in South Sudan. Due to the high rate of illiteracy there are early pregnancies which sometimes result in death.

There are some forced marriages by the members of the liberation struggle as well as by the enemy soldiers. The war has resulted in separation of families and relatives and a lack of peace and tranquillity not only in the communities but also in individuals' lives. People's assets have also been destroyed or sometimes confiscated. There has been unemployment. All this renders the society seriously incapacitated and the people traumatized.

---

4. International Crisis Group, *God, Oil & Country*, xi, xii, 115.
5. *Hope: A News Letter of the New Sudan Council of Churches Issue No. 8 January/February 2000*, 7.

The Southerners themselves also practice tribalism, which is why there are tribal conflicts. Some individuals among the displaced communities in South Sudan also herd their cattle in the fields of the indigenous people. When the owners of the crops complain, it results in conflict.

The South has suffered its own wave of internal conflict, strife, confusion, division, self-betrayal, and self-destruction. Some of its people have witnessed, experienced, and suffered violence (78%), rape (74%), murder (48%), robbery (80%), and many other evils in the hands of their own brothers. For instance, in Wau, a man who tried to stop a gang from raping his daughter was forced to lie down, and the gang raped his daughter on top of him.[6] Seeds of bitterness, anger, revenge, and total hatred have been planted among tribes and regions. All these internal wounds will not allow true peace to take hold in South Sudan unless they are healed. People feel that if true peace is to be attained then justice must take its cause and the Southerners must reconcile themselves to one another[7]

The people of South Sudan and those in the marginalized areas have gone through many experiences during the conflict in Sudan. This makes people feel that the perpetrators should be exposed and prosecuted so that peace with justice may be firmly established. The South Sudanese have suffered for too long. They hope after their suffering, justice, and peace will come.[8] With these bitter memories, how easy is it to bring about reconciliation? Is it meaningful to talk of restoration given the bitter past experiences and memories? How easy will it be for those grossly affected by the conflict to forgive and reconcile? People respond to these questions differently. Reconciliation could be easy for some but not for others. Others feel it depends on whether the offender is repentant or not.[9]

All the Sudanese have been yearning for immediate, just, and sustainable peace. That is, an era of responsible, just, transparent, people-led, and

6. Life and Peace Institute, *Peacebuilding Workshop Training for Sudan Council of Churches—Khartoum, Sudan March 15–16, 2004* (Nairobi: Life and Peace Institute, 2004), 31.
7. Hope, Issue No. 1, 1998, 10.
8. Peter Hammond, *Faith Under Fire in Sudan* (South Africa: Frontline Fellowship, 1996), 113.
9. Life and Peace Institute 2004, 31.

integrity-based governance. The country should be founded on the values of justice, democracy, good governance, respect for fundamental rights, and freedoms of individual, mutual understanding, and tolerance of diversity within Sudan as a whole. The parties to the conflict should continue to resolve the root causes of the conflict and violence in Sudan which inflict hardship and suffering on the people of Sudan and seriously hampers the prospects of economic development and social justice in Sudan. This will lead to peace and stability, delivery of essential services, and sustenance of justice and peace for and between the citizens of Sudan.[10]

By peace we do not mean mere absence of war or cessation of hostilities but a just and durable peace where people can enjoy their human rights and where the pursuit of happiness, freedom of expression, worship, freedom of movement and association, and self actualization are respected.[11]

5.3 People's Views of the Peace Talks and Agreement

The people believe that to achieve a lasting peace there is need for addressing the root causes of the war.

Seventy-six percent of the respondents regard the peace agreement as valuable, because it would end a long period of suffering and usher in a period of peace in South Sudan and Sudan at large. They also consider the agreement genuine because it has both regional and international guarantees and safeguards. These people argued that the six protocols addressed the real causes of the war. Therefore, if the peace agreement can be implemented it will grant the Southerners freedom, equality, and justice they have always cherished and struggled for in many years.

> . . . the six protocols enumerated in this declaration shall, if carried out honestly, diligently with unfailing political will,

---

10. *Protocol Between the Government of Sudan and the Sudan People's Liberation Movement on Sharing Power, Naivasha, Kenya, Wednesday May 26, 2004 and State House, Nairobi June 5, 2004, Nairobi Declaration of Final Phase of Peace in the Sudan.*
11. David Mozersky and John Predergast, "*Sudan: peace can change the Country.*" Sudan Mirror, October 27–November 2, 2003:18.

regenerate the Sudan and settle its fate as a country voluntarily united in justice, honor and dignity for all citizens and for the first time since independence. The agreement will change the Sudan forever! Sudan cannot and will never be the same again as this peace agreement will engulf the country in democratic and fundamental transformation instead of being engulfed in war as it has always been up to the present.[12]

5.4 The Six Protocols: An Overview

The six protocols in order of signing are:

1. The Machakos Protocol of July 20, 2002.
This protocol states a referendum would be held after six years and six months to determine whether Southerners would need unity or separation. That Sharia Law would only be practiced in the North while South would be free from Sharia.

2. Agreement on Security Arrangements signed on September 25, 2003.
The protocol on security arrangements recognizes the existence of two armies that had been fighting themselves for twenty-one years as a national army. The SPLM/A will be an army of Sudan in the South and Sudan People's Armed Forces will be Sudanese army in the North. There will be a unified force of 24,000 soldiers comprising of equal proportion of the SPLM/A and the Sudan People's Armed Forces.

---

12. John Garang De Mabior, "Speech on the Occasion of Signing of the Nairobi Declaration on Launching the Final Phase of Peace in the Sudan." State House Nairobi. June 5, 2004.

3. Wealth Sharing signed on January 7, 2004.

The wealth sharing protocol states that 50 percent of oil revenues and non-oil revenues will go to the South and 50 percent will go to the North during the interim period.

4. Power Sharing signed on May 26, 2004.

The power sharing protocol states that during the six years and six months Umar el Bashir will be the president of the Republic of Sudan and John Garang will become the first vice president. There will be four layers of government: county, states, regional, and national government. Thirty percent of those who participate in the national government will be from the SPLM/A. In the government of South Sudan 70 percent will be from the SPLM/A, 15 percent from any other political party in South Sudan, and 15 percent will be apportioned to Southerners in the national congress party.

5. Resolution of Conflict in the Kordofan / Nuba Mountains and Blue Nile signed on May 26, 2004.

This protocol states that these two areas will also be governed in a special way by a government made up of 45 percent SPLM/A and 55 percent national congress party in a rotational governorship in the first three years of the interim period.

6. The Protocol on the Resolution of the Abyei Conflict signed on May 26 2004.

The protocol on Abyei County states that Abyei will get a special status under the presidency of the President of the Republic and the President of South Sudan during the interim period.[13]

The Peace Agreement claims to be anchored in democratic and constitutional guarantees of freedom and equality of all citizens, which will create conditions for peaceful coexistence, mutual dignity, equality, justice, security, and economic development.

---

13. The National Working Group for Civic Education (NWG-CE)–Protocols Dissemination. The Six Protocols: A Summary Booklet, 2–17.

Some analysts view these protocols as representing a compromise between the Sudan government and the SPLM/A and according to some South Sudanese, all issues of the conflict have been addressed by these protocols and what remains are only the modalities for implementation.

The researcher holds the view that a genuine peace process is one which steps out to resolve the fundamental questions that provoked the conflict. Therefore, there is need for full respect and implementation of the peace protocols in order to guarantee lasting security, justice, and equality for all in Sudan. However, the promotion of peace is a task requiring the conversion of hearts, for agreements and treaties cannot alone guarantee a lasting peace. Feelings of bitterness and suffering cannot be made to disappear by means of mere political agreements. Besides, human rights violations or atrocities committed during the war are not addressed by the protocols. In this case, the Comprehensive Peace Agreement seems to have forgotten issues of individual justice. It speaks a great deal about reconstruction but very little about reconciliation.

The parties agree to initiate a comprehensive process of national reconciliation and healing throughout the country as part of the building process. Its mechanisms and forms shall be worked out by the government of national unity.[14]

The researcher fears that the occasion of national reconciliation might be used by the Sudan government for campaigning for Southerners to vote for unity during the referendum. Also, the government will embark on reconstruction and less on reconciliation; yet both are aimed at solving different issues. Reconstruction deals with rebuilding infrastructure, not so much about reconciling. While it is true that infrastructures had indeed been destroyed and need reconstruction, reconciliation is equally important and urgent because it has to do with something more delicate and basic: the reconstruction of the social fabric, brutally torn by the war.

The researcher holds the view that the work of promoting peace is very wide, it is not just about signing of agreements. Sudan's history contains

14. *Protocol Between the Government of Sudan and the SPLM on Power Sharing Signed on 26th May 2004.* (2004). Available at: http://www.splmToday.com/my/nc/downloads/power_sharing.doc. Viewed on February 20, 2005.

a powerful example of peace agreement that failed to bring about peace that was deep enough. The Addis Ababa Agreement is still one of the few examples of a mediated settlement to a long civil war. This was insufficient to make a lasting solution to Sudan's problem. It was not implemented but suffered a violation in word and spirit and was finally abrogated. This was what led to the conflict just being resolved. Due to this, the government and the people of South Sudan should learn from experience and bear in mind that they are dealing with yet another regime that does not respect or honor agreements and covenants it enters into with other parties. Hence this agreement reached should be approached with utmost care and vigilance until the results of the referendum will be out.

5.5 Methods of Forgiveness

5.5.1 Unconditional Forgiveness of Perpetrators of Crimes

The respondents held different views concerning issues of reconciliation, peace, and justice. Fifty percent of the respondents agreed that the government of South Sudan should grant amnesty to the perpetrators of injustice or those who committed atrocities during the war. They argued that what happened in Sudan was that of a guerrilla war and a situation different from that in South Africa during the apartheid, hence it does not require the setting up of a truth and reconciliation commission. That those who committed atrocities should just be forgiven and people should open a new chapter. Otherwise, those who committed crimes were too many and it could be difficult to try them. Some of the offenders were senior ranking officers who would be placed in high leadership positions in the government of South Sudan. In this case, the imperatives of peace and justice may be in conflict because if they were brought before a court for trial, the people they were intended to lead would never respect them.[15]

---

15. Stanley Lo-Nathan, Personal interview, October 13, 2004.

They further argued that the South Sudanese should recognize their existence and learn to live together without destroying themselves. They need to solve their differences and live in unity. For peace is the responsibility of the South Sudanese communities and therefore they should forget what had happened during the war and accept to live with one another and heal the wounds inflicted on them by rape, murder, torture, etc., during the war. And they need to do this openly so that reconciliation and peace can happen. This is the work of the civil societies, the government, NGOs, the churches, youth, and men and women.

If these issues are not addressed as soon as possible, it is feared that the people of South Sudan will not live at peace. For true peace will only come when people forgive one another. In this case, the peace agreement is a first stage which helps people come together to build peace, otherwise with war raging on, things cannot move. So the hostilities have to cease altogether before South Sudanese can embark on discussing true peace and reconciliation. In addressing the issues of rape, murder, etc., these issues must be addressed at all levels because even if the government is going to announce an amnesty that will not heal the wounds in people's hearts and minds. For this reason, the civil society has to set up a peace and reconciliation committee to address these issues. South Sudanese should ask themselves whether they should take revenge or forgive. Will revenge help them? Revenge and counter revenge will never help them. But unless awareness is created revenge will happen. Besides, seeking for strict justice might slide into revenge and keep the cycle of violence on going. As such, people should learn to forgive and reconcile in order to live in peace and harmony. There is need for professional approaches because killing and revenge will only perpetuate the cycle of violence.

This view holds that those who committed crimes during the course of the war should be counselled, and they should be ready to say that they are sorry for what they did so that they can be forgiven. It does not say what would happen if they refuse to repent. It argues that somebody has to take initiative to tell them that what they did was wrong regardless of their response.[16] However, it is very vital for the offenders to admit wrongdoing and guilt. This then will be followed by genuine forgiveness by the offended. For true peace in South Sudan, there is need for forgiveness.

The researcher respects the above view but argues that only a true peace would come with a just settlement of conflict. True reconciliation and forgiveness can never come when one of the parties feels unsatisfied with the deal but only when both are at the same level. It is true that violence and revenge will not solve the problems of Sudan. However, the gospel teaches that repentance and forgiveness are necessary to the process of reconciliation. Furthermore, for forgiveness to have a lasting real meaning there must be a full and honest accounting of the facts and public confessions of crimes and other wrongdoings committed during the war. Although individuals may forgive harm done to them, it is not in their power to forgive harm done to others. The church can try to convince people to forgive, but if they want justice, they are entitled to demand it. It is not rewarding to dwell on the painful past and unresolved emotions, but because the past lives on, shapes the present, and threatens the future, the truth should be heard to heal the future as much as the first memory. No true and lasting reconciliation and peace is possible without justice.

5.5.2 Forgiveness with Justice

For forgiveness to happen recognition of what happened is needed. Although forgiveness is needed, punishment of the guilty and some measure of justice are absolutely necessary. For a true reconciliation to take place, some truth about the wrong deeds is to be probed in order to prevent revenge and victimization. This means that forgiveness will only be granted when restorative justice is rendered. So there is no forgiveness without justice.

Thirty percent of the respondents are arguing that those who committed atrocities should be forgiven after justice is done; hence they must be tried in a court of law. These people should be set free after being proved innocent, but they should be prosecuted if found guilty. Unlike the former

---

16. Daniel Deng, Personal interview, Arua on January 3, 2005.

group which advocates for forgiveness without justice, this group urges for forgiveness with justice.

After the cessation of hostilities and signing of a comprehensive peace agreement there would be need for a mechanism similar to a national truth and reconciliation commission because traditional South Sudanese notions of forgiveness and reconciliation may not necessarily correspond to the standards of national or international law. In this case they recommended that an indigenous truth and reconciliation commission be set up to hear the reports of victims and call the offenders to account. This is because there were individuals who killed others out of the killers' own personal grudges against the victims. For this reason criminals should not be given blanket amnesty. Offences should be weighed because there are those which deserve punishment, others forgiveness while others deserve imprisonment of the offender. Serious offenders should be brought to justice to avoid tribal feuds and to deter others from committing similar offences. Similarly, punishing the offenders will strengthen the rule of law. As such there is a need to set up a proper administration to deal with the people who committed crimes so that victims of atrocities do not seek revenge. Amnesty could only be granted to political detainees because they served the orders of their superiors. It is also argued that those who committed serious crimes during the war should not be entrusted with public offices. According to this view, for true peace to return to South Sudan there is need for reconciliation based on justice, equality, and unity among Southerners.

The researcher concurs with this group because he believes that forgiveness and reconciliation is based on justice. There is need for justice for all marginalized and oppressed people of Sudan including the victims of atrocities during the war. If this is done, peace and harmony will be sustained in the long term. If the war was a struggle for justice, freedom, and equality and if this has been won at the negotiating table, then there is also a need for individual justice. For a true reconciliation to take place, some truth about the wrong deeds needs to be probed in order to prevent revenge and victimization. Justice has to be added to peace and reconciliation. The issue of amnesty can be considered later after justice and truth has been uncovered. The perpetrators must acknowledge what they did and repent so that they can be forgiven. This is why a truth and reconciliation commission may be appropriate as it is a necessary component of peace building. This should not be understood to mean provoking of the conflict anew, but rather it is a process that will help promote reconciliation and peace. It should not merely be the judging of the perpetrators but also a means of compensating the victims. It is mandatory for the public to know what happened, how it happened, and why. A frank admission of wrong will help both victims and perpetrators to live together and have nothing to fear. It is true that it was difficult to impose law and order during the armed confrontation. During such time crimes commonly went unpunished. But now that a peace agreement has been signed, subjecting the perpetrators to the due process of a formal judicial system should break this cycle of impunity. Every effort should be made to codify and enforce punishments that will act as a deterrent for crimes. People should be held accountable for their crimes. Indeed prosecution of violators of human rights would conform to the principle of justice and meet the needs of the abused communities and individuals, but the dilemma is whether reconciliation would be achieved if key figures were at risk of imprisonment.

5.5.3 Forgiveness and Compensation

There are those who suggest that to restore interpersonal relationships broken by atrocities committed during the war there is need for both forgiveness and compensation of the victims. When the government sets up a compensation policy, the aggrieved party will easily forgive their offenders. This is to render justice to the victims.

This is a sound view because since time immemorial, all communities in South Sudan have their own differing methods of conflict resolution. Reconciliation has deep roots in the people's history and culture. It is conducted at various levels of society and was necessary for settling disputes and resolving conflicts. There is compensation by the offending party depending on the nature and magnitude of the dispute or conflict. Such compensation is to stop the cycle of revenge and violence especially in case where life has been lost. Compensation is done in kind by giving between thirty and fifty cows for intended murder and fifteen or twenty-five cows for manslaughter among the Dinka communities. When compensation failed, revenge would follow. The aggressor would be killed.[17] While in other tribes it would be in terms of goats. There were cases in which a young lady was given to the family of the victim to produce children for the late. Still in others, compensation was not considered necessary as no number of animals or any quantity of materials given would be worth the value of the life or lives lost. When compensation is accepted and done, there is reconciliation marked by slaughtering of an animal which is cooked and enjoyed by the conflicting parties as a sign of oneness, togetherness, harmony, and reconciliation. This symbolizes permanent forgiveness, trust, and covenant. It further strengthens the restored peace and love that comes with reconciliation. Indeed efforts at local reconciliation between neighboring ethnic groups are fundamental to providing an atmosphere more conducive to a lasting peace.

Some people may think compensation is not Christian, however, it agrees with the biblical concept of restitution clearly elaborated in Exodus 22:1–15.

The New Sudan Council of Churches has been instrumental in promoting what it calls "People-to-People Reconciliation" to quell intraethnic and interethnic conflicts, and it has been effective. One such conference led to the Dinka and Nuer tribes signing a peace covenant in March 1999 after seven years of blood bath caused by interethnic violence between them. At the end of the Conference a white bull (mabior) was sacrificed to take away "that which divided us" as put by the traditional spiritual leaders. The slaughter of the white bull signified peace and reconciliation. They concluded by agreeing to let bygones be bygones and joined hands to resolve urgent matters of common interest amicably.[18]

However, there is inability of the traditional procedures to manage certain forms of violence. As such traditional authorities find it difficult to restrain individuals who are from other areas of the country if they do not feel they are subject to local rules of conduct. Yet recognition needs to be

---

17. Peter Mayen and Malual Agan, Personal interview, on October 16, 2004.
18. Esther Wani, "Dinka and Nuer sign peace covenant." HOPE, Issue No. 3. March / April 1999: 7, 8.

given to the traditional procedures and a way should be sought to strengthen their authority that local communities can bring in terms of tradition.

5.6 The Role of the Church in Reconciliation and Peace

Ninty-four percent of the respondents strongly agree that the church has a role to play in bringing about reconciliation and peace in South Sudan by preaching the message of reconciliation and forgiveness and by advocating for justice. The church has a moral responsibility and authority to bring reconciliation between people and people and between people and God using the cross as the basis of reconciliation. Throughout the long war many people have turned to God and therefore through the church's preaching many will learn to forgive. Experience has shown that for reconciliation to hold, the church's involvement is paramount. It should therefore hold a workshop on peace and reconciliation aimed at uniting the divided communities to build peace. The church should also defend human rights of all and emphasise its teaching on repentance, forgiveness, love, joy, unity, justice, and peace: this will foster a true spirit of reconciliation. It has to get involved in peace education and reconciliation based on the Bible so that the communities are transformed.

They also argued that the church has the responsibility of uniting the South Sudanese by preaching the message of forgiveness, reconciliation, and love. The church deals with forgiveness, reconciliation, and love other than revenge, punishment, and imprisonment. That the church in Sudan should play an advocacy role and enhance conflict resolution programs among ethnic groups or tribes. It has to transform people's attitudes and behaviors, and create awareness for societal change while at the same time ensuring equality of all and advocating for peace with justice. They further said that the church would succeed because it commands the people's respect although some politicians hate it for reasons best known to them. This would heal the wounds created during the war. The church has to organize peace and reconciliation workshops. It should also train competent biblically based counsellors who will actively participate in peacemaking at the individual, community, and national levels by counselling people. The church has to promote peaceful coexistence among South Sudanese.

The church has played a significant role in the management of the Sudanese conflict. It has initiated what it calls People-to-People Peace Process which has brought reconciliation among different tribal groups in South Sudan. This has transformed conflict situations and improved relations between warring factions. It acted as the conscience of the movement and condemned atrocities committed against the people. These achievements can serve as positive indicators of hope for the future. However, the church has to garner resources and unite in order to face the present challenge of reconciliation.

5.7 The Role of the Government

5.7.1 The Role of the Government of South Sudan in Reconciliation and Peace

The respondents accept that the Government of South Sudan has a role to play to bring about peace by establishing the rule of law and practicing democratic governance and justice. To bring about reconciliation to South Sudan, the government of South Sudan should punish wrong doers. If it is going to grant amnesty to those who committed atrocities during the war, it should set up a policy to compensate victims so that they can forgive and a new page can then be opened for everybody to start a new over again. This will help people to live together in harmony. The government has to enforce law and order, give freedom to all, and treat all its citizens equally. For true peace in South Sudan there is need for administration of justice to all. For if there is justice, further conflicts will be avoided. There is need for equal distribution of wealth, services, and employment opportunities which should be granted on merit and not on tribal basis. Transparency and democratic governance are also necessary for a peaceful South Sudan. There is need for a government structure which is representative of all Southern tribes and leaders should be democratically elected. People should be treated justly and their human rights observed. The government in conjunction with the church should also create peace education program for conflict resolution.

5.7.2 Separation of South Sudan from the North

Still for others the surest way to bring about true peace to South Sudan is to separate South Sudan from the North. This, they argued, is the only solution to the South Sudanese problems because they have lived with the Arabs for centuries and they know the motives of the Arabs very well. The Arabs do not regard the South Sudanese as equals and fellow citizens due to their religious and ethnic differences. The Northerners are Arabs and Muslims while the Southerners are Africans and Christian or followers of African traditional religions. So there is need to separate the country so that each ethnic group can freely exercise their own cultures. True peace will prevail in South Sudan only if South Sudanese are made to govern their own affairs. Separation will avoid further conflict and reduce Arab monopoly over Southerners and treatment as second class citizens. After all there is no uniting factor that can make both Southerners and Northerners build a nation. Some respondents were so pessimistic that they argued that without separation South Sudanese will again go to war a few years after the signing of the peace agreement because the Arabs are not just and will not respect the peace agreement. Separation is therefore a matter of urgency.

The agreement recognizes the right of the South Sudanese to self-determination, but it seeks to make unity attractive during the interim period.

The researcher, however, observes that although the South is separated from the North, this would not imply that the Southerners would live in true peace among themselves. They have their own differences among themselves. Another fact is that the North will never give up the South because of the natural resources the South has which are not there in the North. As such it will always maintain quasi unity with the South just to maintain its interest even if the South does not benefit from this unity. Furthermore, the Sudanese are diverse and belong to different ethnic, religious, and cultural affiliates, and if they desire to remain united as a nation, they should coexist within that diversity. The foundations of unity in diversity can only be built and guaranteed by pillars of justice and equality for all irrespective of race, religion, tribe, ethnicity, or gender. Therefore the constitutional framework should take into account the special circumstances of each region or state including religion, culture, strategic and economic interests, and rights of self-governance and determination. This it should consider as most appropriate for maintaining the unity of Sudan while allowing each region to exercise autonomy and preserve the specific character of its people.

The researcher now turns to the summary conclusions and recommendations.

CHAPTER 6

Summary Conclusions and Recommendations

6.1 Summary Conclusions

This research has been about the Christian perspective of reconciliation and peace in South Sudan; Sudan was a country gripped in what was set to be, until recently, Africa's longest running civil war. Since its creation, the Sudanese state has been, on many occasions, inherently unjust, repressive, and extremely violent against sections of its own citizens. That was why segments of its people took up arms against it.

There were diverse roots of the conflict which stretch deep into the history and geography of the country. These include historical, political, social, economical, and religious causes. The war had seriously devastated the country with serious loss of lives, displacement, devastated infrastructure, and economy. Besides the major civil war, continuous tribal conflict, cattle raiding, rape, murder, child and women abduction, and forced marriages had been experienced among the tribes in the South. This led to the break down of interrelationships among tribes and communities in South Sudan. There is a widespread feeling of hate and revenge biding for the first opportunity to explode. Now that a peace agreement has been signed, there is a potential of settling of accounts and this threatens the peace agreement.

The research has found out that people have mixed views about reconciliation and peace. All the respondents supported the need for reconciliation and peace, but they suggested various methods of effecting it. The majority argued that the perpetrators should be unconditionally forgiven and people should open a new chapter. While others argued that reconciliation should be based on justice and so the need to prosecute those found guilty. Still for others, there is need for compensation of the victims if the perpetrators are to be forgiven.

The respondents valued the peace agreement and considered it genuine arguing that if it could be implemented it would give a prospect of lasting peace in the country.

However, the agreement did not address the issue of individual justice concerning the atrocities committed during the war. It also focuses on reconstruction more than reconciliation. It lacks any provisions for truth commission, prosecutions, or other forms of accountability for past abuses during the conflict.

The respondents acknowledged the role of the church in reconciliation and peace building. They argued that the church could participate in this task by preaching the message of forgiveness, reconciliation, and advocating for peace with justice.

They also agreed that the government of South Sudan has a role to play in reconciliation and peace building. This, the respondents said, the government can do by setting up a truth and reconciliation commission to bring the perpetrators of injustice into account or compensating the victims; enforcing law and order; treating its citizens equally and justly; equitable distribution of wealth, services, and employment; and exercising democratic governance. The respondents strongly recommended the need for separation of the South from the North, good governance, accountability, transparency, democracy, the rule of law at all levels of government, and equitable representation of all the people in the government as a way of ensuring lasting peace in Sudan.

The general conclusion is that the memories of war are still fresh and raw in people's minds. These memories cannot go away with the signing of the peace agreement. True peace is not just the mere absence of hostilities, but it is based on justice and equality. It is timely to talk about reconciliation and peace because it is a journey and entails time. Therefore, the church, the government, and the civil society should opt for a culture of peace. The church should embark on preaching about reconciliation and peace and advocate for justice. It should encourage traditional conflict resolution and reconciliation techniques and teach on the biblical understanding of peace and reconciliation. While the government should acknowledge the trauma people had gone through, deal with the root causes of the conflict, and address the crimes committed during the war so that the wounds inflicted can be healed for people to live harmoniously with one another.

There is need for South Sudanese to move forward with trust and confidence in order that they can build a just and peaceful country. This calls for national reconciliation, justice, healing, and forgiveness. The Peace Agreement is not only peace on paper, it has to be practical, implemented, workable, and actually resolve the conflict to change people's lives on the ground as well as end the civil war. Reconciliation and justice is the way forward in working out on the implementation of the Comprehensive Peace Agreement.

What then can the church do now that Peace Agreement has been signed? The signing of the Comprehensive Peace Agreement means a great challenge to all South Sudanese towards reconciliation and reconstruction of the nation, in order to render peace effective. The church has to face this enormous challenge of reconciliation so that it does not run the risk of being irrelevant and being an institution with nothing to contribute to the rebirth of her people in a crucial hour of their history. It should therefore have a plan of action so as to contribute in the reconstruction of the nation with special emphasis on peace and reconciliation.

6.2 Recommendations

6.2.1 Recommendations for the Church

To meet its great challenge towards reconciliation and peace building, the role of the church should among other things include:

- Promoting peace and justice.
- Fighting against injustice and inequality by making these an

integral part of evangelism.

- Preaching reconciliation by addressing issues involved in the practical work of reconciliation.
- Safeguarding, defending, and promoting human rights and human dignity as well as making people conscious of their rights and duties.
- Teaching on peace education and conflict prevention for people to handle conflict and reduce violence in the community.
- Involvement in practical community outreach by establishing counselling centers, using the mass media, and holding workshops and conferences to strengthen and support the work of peace and reconciliation
- Rehabilitating politics as a Christian vocation and encouraging Christians to enter politics as a divine calling to help renew the country by evangelising the sinful structures and systems of injustice, corruption, and exploitation.

6.2.2 Recommendations for the Government

There is an enormous undertaking for the government toward an effective rebuilding of the social fabric of the society. Now that a peace agreement has been signed, the government has to resettle displaced persons, refugees, and demobilized combatants. It has to revitalise and re-launch the economy shrunk by war and rebuild schools, health institutions, commercial and other infrastructures destroyed by the civil war. Peace, above all, means promotion of reconciliation between enemies and families who lost their members and goods to violence and whose rights were violated. It means restoring people's dignity and faith in themselves and their destiny. To achieve these, the government should among other things do the following:

- Exercise democracy, the rule of law, justice, and equality.
- Recognize the trauma people have gone through and address the causes for it.
- Disarm and demobilise militiamen and private armies.
- Support community development, resettlement, and rehabilitation programs.

- Respect the dignity and human rights of individuals whatever their race, status, and religion.
- Create an enabling environment for forgiveness, reconciliation, and unity with justice.
- Initiate truth and reconciliation commission to shed light on certain acts that occurred during the war so that reconciliation can succeed.
- Create civic education programs for briefing the citizens of the protocols and the Comprehensive Peace Agreement among other things.
- Support and encourage community based peace initiatives such as the People-to-People Peace Initiatives and the South-South Dialogue.
- Safeguard the Comprehensive Peace Agreement and ensure that it is implemented and not compromised.
- Establish reconciliation and peace building networks in the communities.
- Use TV, radio, and newsletters for disseminating information on reconciliation and peace building programs.
- Enact and regulate laws that govern and streamline grazing areas to protect the interests of both farmers and herders.
- Develop just and fair employment policies and opportunities in accordance with qualification and competence.
- Distribute social services fairly for sustainable development of all communities.
- Initiate policies and training programs for the rehabilitation and welfare of widows, orphans, and disabled persons of the New Sudan, particularly for the war heroes or their orphans and widows.
- Ensure that universal primary education becomes compulsory and is free of charge; and rehabilitate and upgrade all school infrastructures.
- Outlaw abduction of women and forced marriages, and combat rape and sex exploitation of women.

- Protect children from all forms of exploitation and trace out abducted children and severely punish the perpetrators.

6.3 Areas for Further Research:

- The causes of tribal conflicts in South Sudan.
- Reconciliation and peace building between Arabs and Africans in Sudan.
- Forgiveness and compensation.

These areas are important for study so that the root causes of tribal conflicts among South Sudanese can be established and addressed for peaceful coexistence. It is also important to know how the Southerners feel about reconciliation with the Arabs after all that have happened during the war. Furthermore, some people feel compensation is not Christian. It is therefore important to do a study on it. These areas were not covered because they were out side the scope of this study.

APPENDIX

I. Personal Details

I am a student of Master of Arts in Theology at Uganda Christian University. I am writing a thesis on the Christian perspective of reconciliation and peace in South Sudan. I am interested in finding out whether the end of hostilities in Sudan will mark the end of interpersonal, group, tribal, or interethnic conflict. Or there is a lot more that the church and the government in Sudan as well as the people of Sudan need to do in the search for true peace in South Sudan to stop any incidences of violence resulting from revenge. I kindly appeal to you to assist me by answering the following questions as honestly as possible. This will help us find precautionary measures against the emergence of violence which will disrupt our long awaited peace. The information you give will be treated confidentially and used solely for the stated purpose. Answer the questions by ticking the correct answers, and use the papers provided for any additional information.

II. Personal Information

Name: _____

Age: _____

Location: _____

Occupation: _____

Sex: Male _____Female _____

Marital Status: Married _____ Single _____ Divorced _____

Widowed _____ Separated _____

Religion: _____

Tribe: _____

III. Questionnaires

1. List the ways in which the war has personally affected you.
    a. Lack of shelter
    b. Lack of food
    c. Lack of education
    d. Lack of health services
    e. Lack of transport facilities
    f. Inability to exploit development resources
    g. Other (specify) _____

2. How has the war also affected your community?
    a. Lack of clean water
    b. Poverty
    c. Disruption of social life
    d. Destruction of infrastructures
    e. Death of prominent community members
    f. Other (specify) _____

3. Are the peace talks in Naivasha valuable?
    a. Yes
    b. No
    If Yes, say why _____
    If No, say why _____

4. Do you believe that the peace talks in Naivasha are genuine?
    a. Yes
    b. No
    If Yes, say why _____
    If No, say why _____

5. What do you think would constitute true peace in South Sudan?
    a. Separation of South Sudan from the North
    b. Fair treatment of the Southerners by the Arabs
    c. Administration of justice to all
    d. Other (specify) _____

6. What do you think to happen to bring about true peace in South Sudan?
   a. Complete transformation
   b. Democratic governance
   c. Other (specify) _____

7. What types of interpersonal conflicts have happened in your community?
   a. Rape
   b. Looting
   c. Torture
   d. Killing/murder
   e. Other (specify) _____

8. What, in your opinion, needs to be done to the perpetrators of injustice to rectify the situation?
   a. Forgiveness
   b. Compensation
   c. Revenge
   d. Need for justice to be done, etc.
   e. Other (specify) _____

9. Do you believe the church has any role to play in bringing about reconciliation in South Sudan?
   a. Yes
   b. No
   If Yes, say why _____

10. What can the church do to bring reconciliation?
    a. Preach the message of reconciliation and forgiveness
    b. Advocate for justice
    c. Lead the way in reconciliation by holding workshops
    d. Other (specify) _____

11. What can the government do to bring reconciliation?
    a. Punish the perpetrators of injustice
    b. Compensate victims of injustice
    c. Grant amnesty to the perpetrators of injustice
    d. Other (specify) _____

12. What in your opinion needs to be done to people who committed atrocities to other people?
    a. They should be prosecuted
    b. They should be forgiven
    c. They should be warned
    d. They should compensate their victims
    e. Other (specify) _____

13. Some people are suggesting that everybody should be forgiven. What do you think about the following suggestions?
    a. They should be granted amnesty (be set free)
    b. They should be tried and be punished if found guilty
    c. The government should set up a truth and reconciliation commission to hear reports of victims and call offenders to account

14. What should now be done in order to avoid other conflicts from happening again? The government should:
    a. Treat all people justly
    b. Compensate the victims of atrocities
    c. Punish lawbreakers and criminals
    d. Other (specify) _____

15. What can be done to guarantee true peace in Sudan regarding:
    a. Land
    b. Politics
    c. Natural Resources
    d. People who have lost either relatives or property
    e. Religion

Thank you very much for taking time to answer these questionnaires. May God richly bless you.

Yours sincerely,

Rev. Levi Lukadi Noah
Student, Uganda Christian University, Mukono

III. Interview Questions

1.   How did/do people in your traditional community settle interpersonal or group conflicts which involved shedding of blood or loss of life?

2.   How did/do people resolve those cases which never involved the shedding of blood or loss of life?

3.   Was/is there any compensation by the offending party?

4.   Was/is there revenge on the offending party?

5.   Was/is such settlement regarded effective and binding?

6.   Were/are there resolutions to be adhered to bind both parties to the covenant?

7.   What were/are these resolutions?

8.   Do you believe these ways can still be used today to reconcile groups and or communities in conflict?

9.   Give reasons for your answer.

BIBLIOGRAPHY

Assefa, Hizkias and George Wachira, eds. *Peacemaking and Democratisation in Africa: Theoretical Perspectives and Church Initiatives*. Nairobi/Kampala: East African Educational Publishers Ltd, 1996.

Atkinson, David J. and David H. Field, eds. *New Dictionary of Christian Ethics and Pastoral Theology*. England: IVP, 1995.

Ayoti, Miriam. *Unfinished Business in Upper Nile: Survivor's Account of Aerial Bombardment and Its Effects in the Western Upper Nile—Southern Sudan*. Nairobi: Top Ad Graphs Ltd., February 2000.

Berkhof, Louis. *Systematic Theology*. Grand Rapids, Michigan: The Banner of Truth, 1998.

Blackman, Rachel. *Peace-building Within Our Communities. Roots 4. Roots: Resourcing Organisations with Opportunities for Transformation and Sharing*. UK: Tearfund, 2003.

Boulden, Jane, ed. *Dealing With Conflict in Africa: The United Nations and Regional Organisations*. New York: Palgrave Macmillan, 2003.

Burr, Millard J. and Robert Collins O. *Requiem for the Sudan: War, Drought & Disaster Relief on the Nile*. San Francisco and Oxford: Westview Press, 1995.

Clark, David R. and Robert V. Rakestraw, eds. *Readings in Christian Ethics. Vol. 2: Issues and Applications*. 7th Printing. Grand Rapids, Michigan: Baker Books, 2003.

Elwell, Walter A., ed. *Evangelical Dictionary of Theology. Barker Books*. UK: Paternoster Press, 1995.

Children's Leisure Products Limited. *English Thesaurus*. Scotland: Gedden and Grosset, 2000.

Colleta, Nat J., et al. *The Transition from War to Peace in Sub Saharan Africa*. Washington DC: The International Bank for Reconstruction and Development/The World Bank, 1996.

Colleta, Nat J and Michelle L. Cullen. *Violent Conflict and the Transformation of Social Capital: Lessons from Cambodia, Rwanda, Guatemala and Somalia. Conflict Prevention and Post Conflict Reconstruction.* Washington DC: The International Bank for Reconstruction and Development / The World Bank, 2000.

Eric, Fife S.and Arthur F. Glasser. *Mission in Crisis: Rethinking Missionary Strategies.* London: IVP, 1963.

Fadl, Yusuf Hassan and Richard Gray, eds. *Religion and Conflict in Sudan. Papers From an International Conference at Yale.* Nairobi: Pauline Publications, 2002.

Ferguson, Sinclair B., et al., eds. *New Dictionary of Christian Theology.* Leicester, England: IVP, 1998.

Fisher, Simon, et al., eds. *Working with Conflict: Strategies For Action. Responding to Conflict.* UK: ZED Books, 2000.

Fitzgerald, Mary Anne. *Throwing the Stick Forward: The Impact of War on Southern Sudanese Women.* Nairobi: UNIFEM and UNICEF, 2002.

Gatera, Emmanuel. *The Role of the Christian Church in Resolving Conflicts in Burundi (1962–1997), in African Journal of Leadership and Conflict Management. Vol. 1.* edited by Dr. Nkurunziza R.K Densdedit, March 2002.

Gill, Robin. *A Textbook of Christian Ethics.* Edinburgh: T&T Clark Ltd, 1989.

Hammond, Peter. *Faith Under Fire in Sudan.* South Africa: Frontline Fellowship, 1996.

Hodge, Charles. *Systematic Theology. Vol II.* Grand Rapids, Michigan: WM.B Eerdmans Publishing Company, 1968.

Hudding, Roger. *Bible and Counselling.* Great Britain: Cox & Wyman Ltd, Stoughton, 1992.

International Crisis Group. *God, Oil & Country: The Logic of War in Sudan.* Brussels: ICG Press, 2002.

Life Application Study Bible. New International Version (Michigan: Tyndale House Publishers, Inc., and Zondervan Publishing House, 1991).

Life and Peace Institute. *Peacebuilding Workshop Training for Sudan Council of Churches in Khartoum, Sudan 15th–26th March 2004.* Nairobi: Life and Peace Institute, 2004.

Magesa, Laurenti and Zablon Nthamburi, eds. *Democracy and Reconciliation: A Challenge for African Christianity*. Nairobi: Acton Publishers, 1999.

Majok, Isaac Dau. *Suffering and God: Theological Reflection on War in Sudan*. Nairobi: Pauline Publications, 2002.

Milne, Bruce. *Know the Truth: A Handbook for Christian Belief*. England: IVP, 1982.

New Sudan Council of Churches. *Inside Sudan: The Story of People-to-People Peacemaking in Southern Sudan. A Peace of the People by the People for the People*. Nairobi: NSCC, 2000.

Parker, Russ. *Healing Wounded History: Reconciling Peoples and Healing Places*. London: Darton, Longman and Todd Ltd, 2002.

Prendergast, John. *Sudanese Rebels at a Crossroads: Opportunities for Building Peace in a Shattered Land*. Washington: Centre of Concern, May 1994.

Prendergast, John and Nancy Hopkins. *"For Four Years I Have No Rest": Greed and Holy War in the Nuba Mountains of Sudan. Horn of Africa Discussion Paper Series. Discussion Paper No. 5*. Washington: Centre of Concern, Oct 1994.

Rene, Padilla C. *The Fruit of Justice will be Peace in Transformation: An International Dialogue on Evangelical Social Ethics. Focus on Central America. Vol. 2*. Argentina, America, January /March 1985/86.

Shenk , David W. *Justice, Reconciliation and Peace in Africa*. Nairobi: Uzima Press, 1993.

Shenk, David W. *Justice, Reconciliation and Peace in Africa*. Nairobi: Uzima Press, 1997.

Symposium of Episcopal Conferences of Africa and Madagascar (SECAM) and The Episcopal Council of Latin America (CELAM). *Peace, Fruit of Reconciliation*. Nairobi: Pauline Publications, Africa, 2001.

Tillich, Paul. *Systematic Theology. Existence and Christ. Part III*. London: SCM Press, 1978.

Wink, Walter. *Healing a Nation's Wounds. Reconciliation: A Way to Democracy*. Sweden: Life and Peace Institute, 1997.

Newsletters

"Appeal of the Catholic Bishops of Eastern Africa for Peace in the Sudan." Hope: A Newsletter of the New Sudan Council of Churches. Issue No. 5. July/August 1999.

Wani, Esther. "Dinka and Nuer Sign Peace Covenant." HOPE: A Newsletter of the New Sudan Council of Churches. Issue No.3, 1999.

Lugala, Victor. "Reconciliation: A Case for S. Africa model?" Sudan Mirror. Vol.1 Issue 6. 15th December-28th December 2003: 10.

Mozersky, David and John Predergast. "Sudan: Peace Can Change the Country." Sudan Mirror, October 27th–November 2nd 2003: 18.

South Sudan Post: A Monthly Publication of the Centre for Documentation and Advocacy. 8th Edition. August–September 2004.

Sudan Church Review: The Review of Sudan Church Association. Autumn, 2004.

The Sudan Mirror: For Truth and Justice. Issues 2003–2005.

Olita, Reuben and Agencies. "Sudan Ends 21-Year War." The New Vision, Monday, January 10, 2005:1, 2.

"The Peace Protocals." Sudan Mirror June 28th –July 11th 2004: 1–8.

Yaak, Atem Atem. "Potential Threats to the Agreement: A Different Perspective on Sudanese Issues. " Sudan Mirror. Vol.2 Issue 10. 17th January-30th January 2005.

Unpublished Documents

Janda, Clement. "The Challenge of Christian Ministry in a Post War Sudan." An Address at the Third Graduation Ceremony of Bishop Allison Theological College, Arua, March 27th 2004.

Kwaje. Samson L. The Covenant of the People of Southern Sudan: The Process of South – South Dialogue Launched. SPLM/A Press Release, 21st April, 2005.

Life and Peace Institute, Horn of Africa Programme. Workshop Report. Sudan Church Leaders' Peace Building and Civic Education Held at Jinja Nile Resort-Uganda 4th –15th August 2003.

Maragu, Michael. Conflict Transformation Manual for South Sudan Peace Building Programme (OXFAM, Southern Sudan), 2000.

Peace Documents

Protocols-National Working Group for Civic Education (NWG-CE)-Protocols
   Dissemination. The Six Protocols: A Summary Booklet.

Speech by Dr John Garang De Mabior on the Occasion of the Nairobi
   Declaration on Launching of the Final Phase of Peace in the Sudan (June 5th
   2004).

Reconciliation: A TEE Manual for Church Leaders. A Simple copy for Field
   Testing. Nairobi. MAP International, 2000.

Recommendations and Resolutions of the Chiefs' and Traditional Leaders'
   Conference June 29th to July 12th 2004 at Kamuto, Kapeita County, New
   Sudan.

Together We Remain United in Action for Peace: The Position of the Sudanese
   Churches on the Conflict in the Sudan. Khartoum and Nairobi. 7th July
   1999.

The Sudanese Catholic Bishops' Statement, November 1998.

Transformation: An International Dialogue on Evangelical Social Ethics: Focus
   on Central America (Argentina, January/March, 1985/86).

Internet Sources

American University. *Promoting Justice and Peace through Reconciliation*
   (1990). Available at http://www.American edu/academic .depts/
   acainst/cgy/reconciliation.htmand coexistence alternatives-conference-
   summary=American University. Accessed on 20th January 2006.

The Civil War: Background and Evolution of the SPLM/A (2003). New Sudan
   official website available at: http://www.SplmToday.com./modules.php?name
   splm&page=cvlwar&sect=1. Viewed on 25th February 2005.

The Nairobi Declaration on the Final Phase of Peace in the Sudan (2004). New
   Sudan official website available at http://www.splmToday.com/my/mc/
   downloads/all_protocols_declaration.doc. Viewed on 25th February 2005.

Protocol on Power Sharing (2004). New Sudan official website available at: http://
   www.splmToday.com/my/nc/downloads/power_sharing.doc. Accessed on
   20th February 2005.

The Road to Reconciliation (2001). Available at: http://www.doj.gov.za/trc/legal/
   act9534.htm. Accessed on 20th February 2005.

Promoting Justice and Peace through Reconciliation (2000). American University, centre for Global Peace. Available at: http://www.google.co.ug/search?hlen&ie=130-8859-1 I&q=Reconciliation%2c+Peace and Justice. Accessed on 20th February 2005.

www.ingramcontent.com/pod-product-compliance
Lightning Source LLC
Chambersburg PA
CBHW061042110426
42740CB00050B/2846